Book 7

CAUGHT IN THE CROSSFIRE

**The Dutch in Wartime
Survivors Remember**

edited by

Anne van Arragon Hutten

Mokeham Publishing Inc.

The Dutch in Wartime Series
Book 1 - Invasion
Book 2 - Under Nazi Rule
Book 3 - Witnessing the Holocaust
Book 4 - Resisting Nazi Occupation
Book 5 - Tell your children about us
Book 6 - War in the Indies
Book 7 - Caught in the crossfire
Book 8 - The Hunger Winter
Book 9 - Liberation

© 2013 Mokeham Publishing Inc.
PO Box 35026, Oakville, ON L6L 0C8, Canada
PO Box 559, Niagara Falls, NY 14304, USA
www.mokeham.com

Cover photograph by Manon van Kuijk-Smits

ISBN 978-0-9868308-8-4

Contents

On the front cover

The 'Liberation Monument' in Overasselt consists of three large metal parachutes, set in a field near the small town of Overasselt, just south of Nijmegen.

On September 17 and 18, 1944 supplies were dropped in this field for the headquarters of the 82nd US Airborne Division under the command of General James M. Gavin.

The text on the monument reads:

Landing area paratroopers and gliders
During the liberation of Overasselt
On Sunday, September 17, 1944

The monument was designed by Leo Gerritsen and Henk van Hout. It was unveiled on September 17, 1985.

Introduction

Anne van Arragon Hutten

In response to Tom Bijvoet's call for readers of his newspaper, De Krant, to send in their war memories, a great number of people responded. Some letters yielded only a brief anecdote while other writers sent almost a book's worth of information. Some wrote in Dutch, many more wrote in English. All have proven valuable to this effort to publish first-person, eyewitness accounts of World War ll. We have translated where necessary, sorted and organized, and generally made an honest effort to publish personal memories of life during the war. In the first volume of this book series we examined the invasion of the Netherlands by Hitler's forces. Since then, the various volumes have related stories about learning to live under new rules, how the Nazis dealt with Jews, increasing repression of citizens, the resistance against an occupying power, and the situation in The Dutch East Indies under Japanese occupation.

This book speaks about Operation Market Garden, the massive military battle which saw the Allied forces fighting in vain to push their way into the centre of Holland and into Germany by way of bridges across the Rhine river. The 1977 movie A bridge too far has been widely recognized as telling the story of this battle to a broad audience. Based on a book by the same name (by Cornelius Ryan), this war epic included archival film segments that show the problem of overextended military supply lines which slowed down the Allied advance. It tells how two military commanders, George S. Patton of the USA and England's Bernard Law Montgomery had competing plans for the invasion, with Supreme Allied commander Dwight Eisenhower favouring Montgomery's plan.

The film focused largely on the military aspects of this battle, with generals and commanders, paratroopers and army soldiers dealing with transportation difficulties, location choices for the aerial dropping of troops, and timing of the assault that would put thousands of men well behind German battle lines. The assumption that Hitler's forces would have dwindled to old men and young boys by now caused these military men to vastly underestimate any opposition they might have to face.

Compared to that, this volume of The Dutch in Wartime looks, as did our previous books, at how ordinary Dutch citizens were affected. How would a teenage boy react to the sight of Allied soldiers fighting hand-to-hand with the hated enemy? How did mothers and fathers respond when grenades landed in their neighbourhood or even on their houses? What happened to the villages and towns and cities which found themselves suddenly in the midst of machine gun fire and vicious aerial battles? And if you were the director of a children's home crowded with kids who were essentially orphans, with hundreds of soldiers parked in your street and in your garden, could you remain sane?

These are the stories we want to tell in this seventh volume. You will notice that we include four diaries, the last one quite lengthy. These are contemporary accounts, written by a teenage girl, an eighteen-year-old young man, an accountant, and a mature woman, at the time the events occurred. They are not clouded or warped by memory, but speak the truth as the writers saw it at the time. As such, they are exceptionally reliable witnesses to history, chronicles of the day-to-day experience of living in war.

The Market Garden battle lasted only nine days, but fighting continued during the following months as the Netherlands slipped into the exceptionally bitter weather and deprivation of what became known as the Hunger Winter. But that will be the topic of our next volume.

Historical background

Allied forces that had landed in Normandy on June 6, 1944 had broken out of their bridgehead there after fierce, extended fighting, and soon fanned out across France. Among them were the American 101st Airborne and 82nd Airborne Divisions, the 1st British Airborne, British 2nd Army, and various other British and American forces representing their air forces and army. The Polish 1st Independent Parachute Brigade also played a role. All of them ultimately operated under U.S. General Dwight D. Eisenhower, Supreme Commander of all Allied forces involved in the assault of Fortress Europe. Tanks and troops had made their way across the Seine river with no significant damage to Paris, and by September the northwards march appeared unstoppable. Field Marshal Montgomery's 21st Army Group crossed the Belgian border on September 2 and reached Antwerp two days later. Broadcasts from London's BBC were already suggesting the imminent liberation of the Netherlands, with a false report of the Dutch city of Breda having been liberated.

Certainly the German forces in Holland believed the news. A multitude of soldiers and officers abandoned their positions in panic to head for home by bus, train, bicycle, and even on foot. Armed members of the Dutch Underground sabotaged the fleeing stream where possible, managing to derail at least three departing trains. Dutch civilians rejoiced, prematurely readying flags and orange ribbons, and for one day (September 9, later referred to as Crazy Tuesday) the population celebrated immoderately while jeering the departing enemy. Then came a reality check, with Allied forces stopping in Belgium to consolidate their gains. Montgomery wanted an immediate effort to capture the main Rhine bridge at Arnhem so that this river would no longer pose an obstacle towards securing a toehold in Germany and the advance to Berlin. The plan included a continuation upwards through the Netherlands as far as the IJsselmeer, Holland's great inland sea. This plan, with modifications, eventually formed the basis for Operation Market Garden, the code name for an enormous military action aimed at crossing the Rhine at Arnhem and Nijmegen.

Two distinct operations would be carried out: a massive aerial drop of troops and materiel whose purpose was to capture and secure the bridges across the Meuse and Rhine rivers, and a land offensive with tanks and heavy artillery pushing northward. It was the British 1st Airborne Division which was assigned the task of securing the main Rhine bridge at Arnhem and establishing a bridgehead there. Other divisions were to secure various bridges at Eindhoven, Nijmegen, and nearby towns. The British 2nd Army Division was to invade Holland by way of Eindhoven and Nijmegen towards Arnhem, where they would reinforce the 1st Airborne.

On September 17, more than 10,000 British and Polish paratroopers were dropped into fields surrounding the Rhine, along with jeeps, weapons, gliders, and other instruments of war. The first of them jumped at 1.30 p.m., with about 6,000 landing near Nijmegen and the rest scattered around various towns along the river.

Their specific aim was to clear the way for British tank units which would then continue towards Germany's Ruhr region. Although they succeeded in capturing some of the bridges they ran into unexpectedly heavy resistance from German patrols encountered along the way.

The result was near-total disaster. The 21st Army Group under Montgomery ran into the forces of Field Marshal Walter Model, who commanded the German Army Group B, and happened to be near the landing zone where the Allies had dropped their troops and supplies. He was in charge of an SS-Panzer Korps and was able to requisition reinforcements out of Germany besides, with many heavy tanks at his disposal. It was Model who stopped the Allies in their tracks at Arnhem. Although hard fighting continued in a see-saw pattern for nine days, the Germans vanquished the Allies.

The British, Polish, and American soldiers fought valiantly. By morning of September 18, various groups of paratroopers cleared some German machine gun nests, but German artillery continually challenged their progress. Many houses were heavily damaged or burnt to the ground. In Groesbeek and Mook, more than 3000 troops out of Germany staged a counter-offensive against American forces, with help from another 1300 troops who had survived Normandy. For some time the site of the aerial landing was threatened but the Americans were able to hang on just long enough to allow more gliders with additional troops to land. By late afternoon the Americans were, however, retreating towards the town of Berg en Dal. Meanwhile the British tank division expected to reinforce the aerial attack was late in coming through.

Of the paratroopers who had not been killed, most were captured. Only about 2400 troops, remnants of the 1st Airborne, were evacuated from their location on the north side of the Lower Rhine, with the 20th and 23rd Field Companies of the Royal Canadian Engineers doing most of the heavy work. On the night of September 25-26, they used twenty motorized stormboats, all but one of which sank or was shot out of operation by the end, for the rescue. They had to cross the river, gather a load of paratroopers and head back, in darkness and under continuous heavy machine gun fire from the Germans. The bravery of these Canadians during the 150 river crossings required to evacuate all the trapped survivors eventually won them five decorations, including a Military Cross for Lieutenant Russell Kennedy, reconnaissance officer for the 23rd Field Company.

Nijmegen, only ten miles from Arnhem, bore the brunt of much fighting. Its liberation by the Allies had been a slow process, with the city centre hard hit by fires lit by retreating German troops. Not until the evening of September 20 did the Americans control the city, including the strategically important bridge over the Waal river. Nijmegen was free, but due to the failure in capturing the bridge at Arnhem, the military front now stalled here. With Germans having dug themselves in at Arnhem, the civilian population of the entire region remained in the crossfire for months despite having supposedly been liberated. Hundreds of them died from grenade attacks that shattered homes and plunged into gardens, with many more wounded. Nijmegen remained a front city, tormented by frequent bombings and battles.

True, the Allies had liberated the southern part of

the Netherlands, but that population continued to live under largely wartime conditions. Meanwhile the vast majority of the country remained enslaved. The initially successful march northwards from Normandy had been halted and blocked.

Opinions vary in laying blame for the debacle that resulted from the Allies' unsuccessful attempt to cross the Rhine river and continue north. Some analysts have suggested that the Allies took no notice of reports from the Dutch Underground which knew about a strong German military presence in the area. Regardless of who was at fault, Market Garden, which was the biggest airborne battle ever fought, also became the Allies' biggest blunder and failure of WWll, with terrible loss of life for both soldiers and civilians. Earlier expectations that the Netherlands would be free by Christmas had come to an abrupt end. Meanwhile, the Hunger Winter was beginning its slow, dreadful strangulation of the population, especially within the western cities.

"You're hired!"

André Schabracq

We left Holland in 1942 to live in Paris, where we blended in more easily. We are both Jewish, and during the terrifying days of the German occupation that was a death sentence. I lost my father in Auschwitz concentration camp. Paris was liberated by the American army on the 25th of August, 1944. We were, of course, very happy, although this is not the right word. We were overwhelmed with this new reality of finally being rid of the deathly German occupation.

We were standing on the sidewalk of the Boulevard St. Michel with my brother and some Dutch friends, yelling and shouting in Dutch to each other, when the troops came marching by. With us was an American soldier, who touched me on the shoulder and asked us, "Are you people Dutch?"

It turned out he was of Dutch parents and still used Dutch in church in Michigan. We started a conversation and he told me that his assignment at the moment was to hire people to work for the American army. He asked if I was interested, and inquired about other languages I spoke. I told him, "French, German, English, and of course, Dutch."

"You're hired!" he almost shouted. Three days later I was picked up by two soldiers and taken to Mirecourt, a small town close to Reims. There I was put in officer's uniform with the title of Civilian Technician. My first outfit was with black soldiers, the 377th Engineering Company. Two months later I was transferred to the 151st Engineer Combat Group, and soon thereafter we were on our way to Berlin.

Berlin is another story. Too many new impressions and a totally new experience in the city where the Nazis planned for the Final Solution to the problem of Jewry.

Guiding the 'Tommies'

Charles de Greef

The Battle of Arnhem in September, 1944, was one of the great mistakes of World War ll. My hometown became the place where a war that was almost won, was almost lost. I was there, a 17-year-old schoolboy living only six blocks from the bridge that was the major Allied objective.

September 14 was a Sunday, the day picked as the assault day for the Allied operation called 'Market Garden'. It would launch the greatest armada of troop-carrying aircraft ever assembled, and it would be one of the most daring and imaginative operations of the war. An airborne carpet of Allied troops would be laid across the big rivers of the lowlands, seizing the bridge crossings so that an arrow-like thrust could be launched in a northerly direction into the centre of Holland and the north of Germany.

The top point of this pencil would rest on my home town of Arnhem, a city with a population of 90,000. Arnhem is the centre of eastern Holland, capital of the province of Gelderland, the hub of important railroads and highways, situated on the Rhine river fifteen miles from where the river crosses from Germany into Holland.

I had watched the German paratroopers landing here in 1940. The city became an important air base for German night fighters, intercepting Allied planes on their way to the Ruhr or Berlin. By September of 1944 it became a heavily used escape route for the disintegrating

German forces that were being pushed by the onrushing British and American forces. On September 6 we had experienced what is now called 'Crazy Tuesday', after the BBC of London had spread rumours that the Allies had already entered southern border towns. In a happy mood, people crowded around the southern points of entry, equipped with little English and American flags. They cracked open bottles of Dutch gin that had been saved for the day of liberation and got ready for the end of occupation. When the phantom armoured divisions never showed up, bitterly disappointed citizens hastily withdrew behind their white starched curtains and waited.

In Arnhem we knew that we were a likely candidate for a landing, as we were such an important hub. I lived downtown, where we occupied living quarters above and behind my father's store. Downtown, we had seen a new German element: the cocky black outfits and berets of the notorious SS armoured troops. We soon found that they had picked the woods northeast of town, with their natural cover against air reconnaissance, parking the shot-up remnants of two SS Panzer divisions, the 9th Hohenstaufen and the 10th Frundsberg. These became the complete undoing of the ill-fated operation Market Garden. These units had been mauled badly during the Normandy landings and subsequent rout through France, and only a few dozen tanks were in battle condition. But they would prove adequate.

At 11.00 a.m. in low-level attacks, light bombers came and bombed German army installations, including the main German barracks in the heart of town. It was a neat pinpoint job, but unavoidably demolished the building next door, which was my high school. As it was only six blocks from our home, we were huddling in the basement while jars of preserves rattled and shook. (It also shook a beautiful 15-year-old schoolgirl who lived one block away from the burning barracks. Audrey Hepburn-Ruston was the pride of Arnhem, being its youngest ballerina).

Our first indication of air landings was a hysterical phone call from a cousin who lived on the west edge of town. He shouted: "The Tommies have landed, and they are coming down the highway on little motor scooters!" These were the first pathfinders of the First British Airborne Division, who had picked the heath six miles west of town as their drop area. We rushed upstairs and found our way to the roof and had to hang on for dear life, because the excitement almost pushed three of us off. The sight of hundreds of parachutes way off near the horizon was indescribable. The liberation could not come in any more glamorous delivery, symbolically dropping from the sky. But they landed six miles east of their target instead of right on the bridge.

We saw the 'Tommies' (British soldiers) in our downtown streets. My brother and I quickly met them and found they were looking for the Rhine bridge. We were able to guide them towards the river, avoiding the main streets and staying shielded from some expert German snipers now in the tower of our central cathedral. The spire of this grand old church, in which I was baptized, was a familiar landmark on the Arnhem skyline. The top landing above the belfry was 300 feet above ground level, an excellent observation platform. In the next three days it would change hands seven times, and on the fourth day it would be weakened by direct artillery hits, causing fires in the 17th-century wooden beams, until it stood like a huge hollow torch.

But on the night of the 17th, the Tommies were with us, exuding confidence and loping through the street, fighting as if it were a soccer game. Many discarded their helmets and donned their proud maroon berets. Our house was right in the middle of the street fighting and sniping. The din of whistling and zinging bullets was all around us.

That evening our family started to look for a safe place to spend the night, so we made our way into the building behind us. It was a big provincial bank, and the caretaker lived behind the lobby. He let us in and we set up quarters in the basement vaults. That must have been the most luxurious bomb-proof quarters in town. Food preparation still had to be done in our own kitchen, and my mother would brave the warfare to take advantage of the gas supply that still lit our stove. To stay below window level, her activities between sink and stove had to be undertaken on all fours.

On Monday, we were still able to direct some of the British liberators. But already things had become risky, dodging and running along the houses, and the first casualties started to dot the streets and alleys. There was no doubt about it now, the Germans were coming back in. They had regrouped and they had tanks. The danger of this numbed us because we knew that our British friends were not equipped to fight against armoured columns. We had seen our first jeeps; some of the paratroopers had bazookas, but they could not prevent the wedge that the Germans drove between the battalion that had occupied the bridge in the meantime, and the drop zone west of town.

By afternoon, very few of the airbornes could get through to reinforce their mates around the bridge. Peering through the windows we saw more and more Germans coming through, shuffling from door to door in an array of uniforms that ranged from Waffen SS to Navy to green helmets. They were an odd lot, scraped together from broken-up units, but they were striking back. With resilient improvisation, the local commanders had worked all night in an effort to take back Arnhem.

Monday night we tried to get some rest in our vaults, but the Germans were already banging on the doors, looking for hiding Allied paratroopers. The block east of us was Nazi-controlled by Tuesday morning, and they wasted no time. In rounding up civilians they found four brave citizens actively assisting our liberators, and a small platoon of SS fanatics marched them into the garage of a storage company and executed the four against the wall. Among them was a prominent doctor who was also head of the Red Cross in our city.

Some thirty miles south of town, struggling for every mile of their northbound attack, were the British tanks that were supposed to roll into Arnhem, make the connection, use the bridge, relieve the hard-pressed little band of paratroopers, liberate the city, and speed eastward into the German plains. But the weather turned bad, heavily overcast with poor visibility, so delivering supplies from the sky was delayed by a whole day. In the meantime, the Germans had gotten into position around the landing and drop areas. Supplies were being dropped by parachutes in large five-foot containers.

The Dakotas came in low and ran into heavy German fire, which forced hasty and inaccurate drops. Most of the supplies fell into German hands, and the frustrated Tommies could only watch helplessly. The next twenty-four hours were depressing. Our part of town was retaken, and the only British around were dead in the street, heavily bandaged on stretchers, or nudged along as prisoners of war. Under these circumstances it was obviously necessary for young lads like myself and my brother to get out of the way. The Germans were becoming round-up happy about able-bodied citizens, and so we had to leave the parental home, the safe vaults and the un-liberated part of town.

We loaded our bicycles, put on an extra suit over the one we wore, and installed little white flags on the handlebars of our two-wheelers. As we were too shaky to pedal, we pushed the bikes up the street, naively trusting that the white pennants would cease all crossfire and safeguard us out of town. With heavy feet we trudged along the familiar blocks which now seemed five miles long, in dazed amazement that none of the stray bullets had cut short our evacuation. The further north we got, the more solidly German the strongpoints became, and the more we realized that our liberation had lasted for only thirty-six hours, and that the brave friends of the airborne division were surrounded, pushed back, and hopelessly lost.

Their pockets of resistance would last another week, and on September 25, Major-General Roy Urquhart would withdraw the remains of the proud unit that had fought for the Arnhem area, in a night escape across the Rhine. In all, some 10,000 men had been dropped or had landed by glider, but only 2,200 would escape. The rest was left behind, including 1,200 dead and 6,600 missing, wounded, or captured.

A heavy toll was taken by the Dutch population. Two brothers who were in high school with us had also roamed around with British units for several days. They had picked up abandoned British helmets, which they proudly wore, along with other stray pieces of equipment and pouches. While making their way home through the woods, they ran into a group of trigger-happy Germans. The equipment must have labeled them as British auxiliaries. Without further trial or examination, the lads were set up against some trees and shot dead.

A week after the landing, on September 24, the local German Kommandant decided that Arnhem was a front line position and that the civilian population was only in the way and hindering the orderly battle. He ordered the evacuation of the entire population within twenty-four hours.

The road of suffering for the citizens had only just begun, and most of them could only take along what they could carry in a handbag, suitcase, or on a bicycle. Green and inexperienced RAF pilots mistook the gray columns, trekking northward, for escaping Germans. The tragic mistake of low level strafing took many lives and confused a good many burghers about who was liberating them. Two weeks after our fine city had been turned into a ghost town, a limited number of citizens were allowed each day to go back to their houses on a six-hour pass.

The Allied action had ground to a halt, and not until May 1945 would Canadian troops truly liberate our city and march through its empty avenues. The many months of German looting had turned Arnhem into a true ghost town, and my family never had the heart to go back, start anew, and pick up the pieces.

Birthday in a cellar

Anthony van Kempen

My parents, four brothers, two sisters and I lived at 65 Spoorstraat (Railway Street) in the town of Boxmeer, North Brabant. Our living quarters, a bakery and a grocery store were on the main street. In 1944, our occupation by the Germans seemed to be coming to an end. My father woke us up one time to look at a retreating army.

There were trucks pulled by horses, full of pigs, sheep and cattle, all taken from farms. Another day we woke to find a cannon across the street from our store. We watched as the Germans loaded the gun and pulled the rope, and fire spewed out. The reply came from the road to St. Anthonis. The Allied forces fired back and the Germans fled. Then came what is now known as Operation Market Garden.

It was the 17th of September, shortly before my 10th birthday. The sky was full of parachutes with soldiers, small trucks and jeeps. It was a spectacle I will never forget. A fighter plane buzzed overhead and started firing on the locomotive of a train on its way to Germany. Suddenly the engine boiler spouted steam and the train slowed to a halt. The engineer jumped out and dove into the ditch. Tanks pulled into town and were stationed on the railroad tracks and the main road to Beugen. British and Canadian troops were everywhere.

Some Germans threw out their guns from their hiding places at the coal distributor and were taken away. Other Germans were fleeing across the fields into the bush. All this time there was shelling all around us and we would go and look at the damage being done. The house across the street was severely damaged. Our eyes couldn't see enough of all that was going on around us. The news came that two boys were seriously injured, and later died. We were rounded up.

My parents decided to sleep in the cellar overnight. Every day my father would go out to see what was happening. Each day he returned safely. I remember mother commenting that we would surely be safe by my birthday on September 26. But at ten years old I was still trapped in the cellar. On October 1 my father came back and said it was safe. The Allied forces were now in control of Boxmeer. We thought the war was over, but it was not to be. The Allies made the decision to evacuate Boxmeer, since the Germans were not prepared to retreat across the river Maas. They kept coming back into town at night to plunder. My three brothers, one sister and I were given a bag of clothing and told to retreat behind Allied lines. Since we had relatives in Rijkevoort we headed there. My parents decided to go later by bicycle. They took my youngest sister and brother and other belongings. As we were walking the shelling started again. We were forced to take shelter in the bush behind a farmhouse. But we arrived safely at my uncle's place.

Liberation of Eindhoven

From the diary of Liesbeth Boysen

n 2011, Liesbeth Boysen's teenage diary was translated by
her husband for their children. Her almost daily entries,
condensed for this book, began one day before the liberation
of Eindhoven on Sunday, 17 September, 1944. Liesbeth was
fourteen years old. Her diary shows how life went on for
civilians south of Holland's great rivers once they had been
freed. In the north, the population was still starving.

Sunday, September 17, 1944

This morning when I woke up I heard all the flying
aircraft. My brothers and a friend called to me that a
great number of bombers were flying over our house.
I went upstairs. The bombers were dropping bombs in
the neighborhood of Best, about ten miles north of our
house. We went to our neighbors, because they had a
big cellar with two exits. After supper a lot of soldiers
were in front of our house. Suddenly a car came by,
calling out that British soldiers had landed. The German
soldiers fled in a hurry.

Monday, September 18

Everybody came in the cellar; we had slept at Oom
Joop's place. I woke up because there was heavy cannon
shooting. Pappa said we have to leave and go to Janus.
We finally got there with lots of trouble, because the
projectiles and shrapnel were flying over us. We were
there with four families, a really big crowd and very
loud. I saw the British soldiers fighting and the German

soldiers running away in the distance. At 4 o'clock it was announced that we were free. Flags were raised; it was black from all the people at our place.

Tuesday, September 19

Today was the big day! The day of the liberation. In the city it was colossal, the people jumped and danced and sang. An American has filmed everything. Real exciting! The troops went over Franklin Street. What a powerful thing to see. But in the evening I saw flares and fiery bullets and I heard Pappa call and we went in the cellar.

It was terrible, terrible. After a while you could see the city on fire, very frightening. We slept again at Oom Joop's place. There were tanks in front of the door. They were shooting heavily.

Pappa had had been to the hospital in the city, lots of people wounded.

Then I heard from Pappa that Loes van Ketel was dead, I found that very sad, but it was fortunate that Loes's father, mother and sister had died at the same time and place.

Also Mr van Rynstra and his daughter succumbed. The house was bombed and burned fiercely; their cellar window could not be opened. Their fate was terrible, terrible!

Thursday, September 21

Today they are still shooting heavily.

Friday, September 22

I have gone with Mamma to the centre of the city. I was anxious to see Joke Bussemaker, my best friend. They were lucky and all very much alive. Their house is heavily damaged and not livable. There is one place with all damaged houses. At Digna Philips's place there is also a lot of damage; a 40 ton bomb was aimed at their house. It missed but their garden is totally gone.

Saturday, September 23

I went to the funeral of Loes. The sermon was OK, the eulogies were very emotional.

Sunday, September 24

There are many cars and trucks in front of the garage, which is full of soldiers. There is another soldier who played excellently on the piano. Paul has gotten a lot of candies and cigarettes. Last week the Germans were in in that same place.

They are very kind soldiers, and treat us very well. They said that Germany had capitulated, but that was a joke.

Monday, September 25

The troops have departed, but this afternoon we had two other officers sleep in our house. They belonged to the 8th Army with very high trucks.

Tuesday, September 26

We have been free for a week, but in Best there is still hard fighting along the canal and the brick factory.

Wednesday, September 27

The shooting is finished, but it is very busy all around our house. The barricades have been demolished.

We thought they were gods

Greta Stephany

Greta is a sister to Pieter Aarsen whose story follows this one.

It was September 17, 1944. I remember seeing all these things dropping from planes, and it was beautiful. They turned out to be parachutes, and they were not the enemy, but paratroops. We had learned to identify the planes by their colour and the sound. We stood in front of the house and were very excited, screaming and dancing. We thought everything would be alright soon, and we would be free, but that was not so.

That Sunday we were in church. We started hearing noises above us, like planes shooting at each other, and flying low. We knew that meant we had to find shelter, but the minister kept preaching as usual. People became restless and there was lots of whispering. Then, all of a sudden, we heard bombs falling. Everybody got up and started running outside, to our homes, and safety, or so we thought and hoped. It was routine to hide in our cellars, but we did not have time. I see us in the kitchen, being afraid. We hear the planes and the deafening noise. I see my sister running around the kitchen table, and my mother screaming at her to lie down, but she went crazy, and kept running in total panic, and fear. Our grandma was praying out loud. My father and mother were lying on top of us, under the kitchen table. There is more noise all around us, and shooting again from the ground. My father 's eyes were big and full of fear. I had never seen that, and never did again.

We did get in the cellar, because I see a woman come down our stairs, being carried by men. My father was a nurse in our psychiatric hospital, and he was washing her wound, when she was lying on the cellar floor. Still there are planes coming over, very low, and more bombs are falling. The noise was terrible. It took a long time, and then it stopped.

We must have been able to go outside, since I see my father running now, to the train station. Apparently, to see what the damage was, and help the wounded. The heartbreak was yet to come, when we realized how bad it was. One hundred people died that day in our small village of Wolfheze.

The reason for the heavy bombing was the ammunition which the Germans had piled up on the hospital grounds. They did not care about civilian lives. We also had trains coming and going with military hardware. The Germans had occupied our town for a long time, and even if we were used to them, we feared them with all our being. and that fear was constant.

One day I saw our school principal walking on the road, all alone, coming from a direction where the Germans were housed. They had tortured him for information about the Resistance. I clearly, even now, see him walking from where they had held him. His eyes where blank and dull, and he was not walking right. He looked like he had lost his mind, and he never recuperated from that.

We also heard rumors that a boy was killed who would not give information to the Germans. He had been hiding, but they caught him, and he was shot execution style. We went to the same school. He was older than I am, and the Germans wanted those boys for the labor camps. He was my brother's friend, and came to our house often. He worked for the butcher and delivered the meat, on his bike, with a basket in front.

I see, in my mind, our neighbor's boy running into our kitchen. His eyes were big and terrified. He was screaming at my father "Mr. Aarsen, hide me, the Germans are chasing me". My father was in the Resistance. My father grabbed him, and they ran outside.

I have an image also of my father, being very hasty and frightened, picking us up one at a time, and throwing us over the fence in the backyard, where the woods were, and the pig sty. He told us to run! Later we heard that there was a train parked at the station, with ammunition. And the Resistance had found out that there was a chance it would be blown up, which meant our town would vanish, and everyone with it. But it did not happen.

We had been in the woods for most of the day, in a ditch, to find shelter from the bombs and the shooting. There was a lot of fighting. We all lay down in that ditch in a long row. It held most of the townspeople. I was next to my grandma, and the last one in the line. Everybody had the cover of trees over their heads, but not me, and I cried so hard, because I could see the sky, and I thought the German planes would see me. But my grandma kept saying not to be afraid. The next thing I see in my mind is German soldiers passing by, walking above our heads. They were young boys, children really. I still see one boy's face, somber and sad, looking down, carrying his rifle in one hand. They passed, and hid in the pine trees.

Then we heard planes again but it was a different sound, not the heavy drone of the German planes. We looked up and everyone got all excited, because they were American. They dragged other planes behind them, gliders. They came down slowly, and landed in the open field next to us, and all the while the shooting continued, from above, and on the ground. We saw the soldiers come out of the planes, running and looking for cover, telling us to be quiet. Our town was ideal for this fighting, since it had woods for soldiers to hide in, and open fields for planes to land.

All of a sudden I look up and see this one American soldier put a tripod right above our heads. He starts shooting over us, towards where the Germans were hiding in the pine trees. I see the bullets flying, back and forth right over our heads. He was kneeling next to the tripod, by a tree. I thought he was the bravest man I had ever seen. His arm was shaking as he held on to this big gun. Grandma screamed at me to keep my head down. Later the American soldiers went to the pine trees and came back with the guns and ammo from the dead Germans, because they had all been killed. I still see them walking, carrying the guns and ammo they had taken off the dead soldiers.

Then the Americans took care of our wounded and gave us food. I remember the chewing gum mostly. We thought they were gods sent from heaven. I see this large man, in his uniform, and all he did was smile and laugh with us, and I never forgot his wonderful handsome face. Of course we did not understand a word they were saying. We watched the tanks and big trucks, cannons, and all kinds of equipment, coming out of those gliders.

One cannon got stuck in the mud, and the townspeople helped to get it out.

Early in the morning, when it was quiet, an American officer told us we should go home. The shooting had died down some. But as soon as we got started, the planes were back and we had nowhere to go. My father would scream at us the word "down!", and we would all fall flat on our faces. Our grandparents were both old and it was hard for them. Opa was senile and stone deaf. He was 6'4" and very stubborn. My parents would try to wrestle him down, and he would fight them, so when they got him down, they would lie on top of him. Our father would do roll call, to see if we were all still there and alive. That day we stayed in the cellar. We got the mattresses from upstairs, and slept on the coal and potatoes.

The next thing I remember was another day of sleeping in the woods. The fighting was still going on and we were safer in the woods. I see us there and hear the children crying. The woman next to us had a wound in her leg and was moaning a lot. In the early morning darkness we started walking towards our home. For some reason my father thought we were free, that the silhouettes we saw in the manholes as we walked by were Americans, so he proudly said "Good morning"! But then the Germans screamed at him and told him to keep moving. It was a shock, and we whispered in fear to each other that they were 'Krauts'.

The Germans did not let us enter our homes, and it would be almost nine months, before we saw our house again. They told us to walk, and they had a sharp point on their rifles, and that's what they pushed in our backs, screaming all the while for us to walk faster. I can still feel that bayonet to this day, and the horror and fear that came with it. Our neighbors were with us also. They had six kids. They made us walk in a long line. Our neighbor kept whispering, "Those are S.S. troops". My dad would say to him, "Shut up or we will all be killed". The S.S. troops were the most feared of all Germans.

On the grounds of the hospital we ended up in the cellar of one of the pavilions. For ten days we stayed in this room, where the furnace and the coal were, and we slept and lived there on top of the coal with two families of nineteen people. It was hard beyond words. Sometimes the bombing would subside, but mostly we heard the terrible noise. One time a piece of shrapnel came clattering down the cement basement steps, outside of that cellar door. We thought it was a grenade, and we really felt we would die. We sang the psalms we had learned, and the more noise, the harder we sang, all together, as a prayer. We could not understand why a Jewish man hiding with us did not sing, but he did not know the words.

Our grandfather slept on the only mattress we had but he got a kidney infection, and my father took him to the church where they housed all the wounded patients. Many of them died, looking like skeletons, because there was very little food, and my father had a dull and haggard look about him whenever we saw him. He and the other men were caring for those patients, so most of the women were on their own with the children. Then the bombing started up again. When the bombs exploded, the fragments would even fly through windows and hit people. One fragment landed in our grandpa's bed, with him in it, along with the Bible that flew from the preacher's pulpit, all in our grandpa's bed! Grandpa himself never got hurt. People called it a miracle, and it was.

There is much to tell about those days in the coal cellar. The last day we were there, we were promised oatmeal by the nurses. We went upstairs for the first time. Part of the building over our heads was destroyed. We sat down in this large room that was still standing, and we sat at a long table, eating the oatmeal. We were black from the coal. My brother was next to me, and I poked my elbow in his ribs. There, on the wall, was what looked like a star. It was a chunk of human flesh, with blood all around it, perfectly centered. I knew I could not eat any more, and we were so very hungry. We never spoke about that to this day.

Then we left and we walked, and we saw the destruction that had happened in those ten days. We came to a very large hole. My father said to walk around it, and we did, quietly. We had seen those holes before. My father's voice was strange. It had been his colleague, and three patients, who had been blown up by the bomb. I looked up and saw the clothes, hanging high up in the tree. I can still see the grey trousers. The clothes were not flat, but bulging with parts of their bodies still in it. Again, we never spoke about it, but it has followed me through my whole life.

That day we left home, not knowing we would not return again until nine months later. Everyone in town went on this journey with no idea where they would end up. It was a long parade of people. The women had covered their heads in white underwear or whatever we could find that was white. The kids carried rags on sticks also. This was so the planes could see that we were civilians. We followed the railroad tracks and walked all day. The Red Cross did whatever they could, and set up checkpoints where we found a place to sleep, all lined up on a bed of straw in a barn.

After ten days of living in the coal cellar, and then walking all day, we did not care, as long as we could lie down. I remember scratching a lot, from the fleas. We walked for two more days, and then some farmers took us in. We stayed with them for three weeks, but due to lack of food we had to move on again. Our parents knew that we should go further north, and I think it had to do with food and shelter. I don't remember too much of that trip, just sitting on a flatbed with a horse in front, and our legs dangling from it.

We came to a city where they put us up with different families. I stayed with a middle-aged couple and their 18-year-old daughter, Inge. Sometimes Inge would take me with her to the soup kitchen, where everyone stood in line for watery soup with cabbage and potatoes. She had a pillow under her skirt so they would think she was pregnant, and then let her go first. One day the woman sent me to the store. As I was walking, the siren went off and everyone ran for cover. There was a garage, and I ran in there and crawled under an army truck. The place had a glass roof, and I was so scared of that glass coming down. There was a German soldier walking around the truck. When he heard me crying, he told me not to be afraid. He kept saying that, in a soothing voice.

Then the all-clear siren went, and I ran home. I lost my shoe. I wanted to go back for it, because that's all I had, but I was too scared, and kept running. I still see a front door open and a woman standing there, with her arms outstretched. She had a big gathered skirt on, and when she sat down and pulled me towards her, I buried my head in her lap, and could not stop crying and shaking. I heard her say to her husband, that my head was ice-cold. Much later we learned that this will happen when someone is extremely frightened.

We had become homeless

Pieter Aarsen

Pieter is a brother to Great Stephany whose story precedes this one.

September 17, 1944 is a date I will never forget. That was the day my village was bombed and many people lost their lives. I was five years old. I do not remember anything of the first four war years; my memory begins on September 17, 1944.

We lived in the village of Wolfheze, about six miles west of the city of Arnhem. My family consisted of parents, four sisters and two brothers between three and seventeen. My father's parents also lived with us, after losing their home along the North Sea when the Germans decided to build bunkers there. There was also a teenage Jewish boy living with us. Life was peaceful, given the circumstance. My parents' biggest concern was Carel, the Jewish boy. They knew it was dangerous to hide Jews but saw this as their Christian duty.

Sunday, September 17 was a beautiful sunny day. Suddenly planes came over very low, and bombs started falling, triggering huge explosions. This lasted about half an hour but felt like a lifetime. We had no time to get into the basement but found cover the best we could. Miraculously we all survived, but 90 people were killed in Wolfheze that day, and many more wounded. The population of our village was about 800. My Dad, being a nurse, rendered first aid but for many it was too late.

We soon heard that the bridge in Arnhem was the

objective in this operation. Heavy fighting erupted between German and British soldiers. We had to leave our house and go into the woods. Soon we, and many of our neighbours, were in a long dry ditch, but the fighting started there as well. The British soldiers, positioned on top of the berm, shot over our heads at the Germans in front of us. We had to keep our heads down and stay in the ditch until early in the morning. On our way home we got shot at again.

The next morning, the Germans told us to get out and line up in the street in front of our house. Our next door neighbours with their six children were also there. We then had to march in front of the German soldiers and become a human shield for them.

My big sister, thirteen years old, had to look after me. She put her arm around me and that's how we walked through the village and over the grounds of the hospital. My brother Harry was taken care of by another big sister. My parents sheltered my grandfather, who had Alzheimer's, between them. Fortunately the British soldiers did not shoot. After some time the Germans told us to get lost and not to return to our house. We did not see our house again until nine months later; we had become homeless people.

For the next eight days the boiler room in one of the hospital buildings became our home. There was no bathroom or running water, and the fighting just would not let up. When things got scary or the noise would get too much for us, someone would say a prayer or we would sing. The neighbour lady was our unofficial choir director. She was always so optimistic, and assured us that if something would happen to us, we would all go to heaven. Years later I asked her if she was never afraid of anything during that time. She said she was always scared but had agreed with my mother that they would never show it in front of the kids.

We saw very little of my Dad or the neighbour dad. They were busy in the chapel, which had been converted into a makeshift hospital for the wounded. The two mothers were responsible for fourteen children between the ages of two and seventeen, as well as the grandparents. After a few days, Dad transferred Grandpa to the chapel because he had come down with a kidney infection and was in terrible pain. We felt bad for him.

Our stay in the boiler room came to an abrupt end when we were ordered to leave. The area would be bombed again, and everyone had to leave. We were fortunate to have a wheelbarrow, with a few blankets and provision. My brother who was fifteen and Carel took turns pushing the wheelbarrow, with us little kids taking turns sitting in it. Our fathers could not go as they had to evacuate with the patients.

During the day-long walk we sometimes had to dive down alongside the road when planes shot at us. We were taken in by a friendly farmer who put us in the barn with the cows and pigs. According to my mother we were too filthy to be put into the farmer's house anyway. We stayed there for about two weeks, and then went on our way again. My mother wanted to reach relatives because she did not want to be a bother to other people. So we packed up and wandered from town to town. Usually my mother would ask for shelter at the local church, and mostly we found a place to sleep. One day Carel disappeared. He had let my mother know that he did not want to be a bother to her any more, knowing how dangerous it was for her to have a Jew with her.

After a while my mother realized that she could not go on wandering with seven children in tow. She made the difficult decision to send the four oldest kids to my Dad's relatives in the Amsterdam area. They made it safely to uncles and aunts. My grandma, who had been with us till then, was taken care of by the Red Cross. My mother, Harry and I, and an older sister walked in the direction of my mother's widowed father. Winter had started. The distance we had to cover can be done in two hours by car today, but we walked for many weeks. We slept where we could. We were always hungry and cold.

We finally arrived at Grandpa's house in Hoogkerk, Groningen. Since Grandma had died a few years earlier, my mother ran the household. Compared to what we had gone through, this was almost like living in heaven. Grandpa had a big vegetable garden, chickens, and goats. The war seemed far away, but one morning a freight train was parked in the railroad yard. We had no idea it was full of ammunition, but the Dutch Underground must have tipped off the Allies. Unaware, my mother left for town. As my brother and I played outside, the sky was suddenly filled with low-flying planes. Shooting started from the ground and the air while bombs dropped out of planes. For my brother and me, this was war all over again. For Grandpa, this was the first time, and he had no idea of what to do. Although I was only five, I ordered Grandpa and my brother into the fruit cellar. At some point I told Grandpa to pray. Grandpa said he couldn't pray with all the commotion, but I insisted and told him that if he didn't pray I would tell my mother. He must have taken me seriously because he said a prayer.

I then insisted on singing, explaining that this is what you have to do when bombs are falling and you are scared. We sang a version of What a friend we have in Jesus, over and over again. When the bombs stopped I suggested we get out of the cellar and run, as the planes would come back. My mother, who was at her cousin's house when the shooting started, ran towards Grandpa's house. A roadblock had been set up and she was not allowed into town. Finally she saw three figures running in her direction: Grandpa, my brother and me. I felt embarrassed with all the hugs and kisses showered on me. Actually we barely escaped death that day. The barn took a direct hit, and Grandpa's house was virtually destroyed in the next bombing run. We never returned there but were taken in by neighbours.

It wasn't until after the war that we were all reunited as a family and allowed to return to our house. We also heard that Carel had made it through the war.

Grenades
were real humdingers

Henk Bosveld

I was born on the east side of Arnhem, at Westervoort. I'm the oldest of four boys in a farm family. I was twelve when the fighting began there. On the 17th of September, a Sunday, I was walking to church, twenty minutes from home, with my grandma when we saw Allied airplanes on the other side of Arnhem, dropping people, dropping vehicles, jeeps. There was some shooting; they were shot at by Germans as they were coming down. It wasn't near enough to us that we had to hide or anything.

Actually it had started for us in August already. My father and I were milking ten or twelve cows in the pasture by hand, about five o'clock in the afternoon, when we saw a dogfight right above us. The German plane came down, burning, and it looked like it came down on our home. We left everything and ran to see what happened. The plane was on the side of a wheat field. I jumped across a ditch, and I just about bumped into a soldier, his pants burning. He was bent over, not lying down. He was dead already. The strange thing was, more people came to look, but we couldn't find pistols or anything. They had probably been taken by the Resistance already. But that burning soldier, I had bad nightmares. I remember screaming that night, and my mother came up. She calmed me down.

We were kicked out towards the end of September and

went to my aunt's. That was about three miles away. There wasn't any fighting then, but the Germans had taken over the farm. We were told to get off the farm and the whole village had to be evacuated. My Dad said to some of the people: "Take a cow with you". We never did get some of them back. They were slaughtered or whatever.

There was just my aunt and her daughter. My Dad and I would walk to our farm to see if there was anything we could save, or get a few apples out of the orchard. The farm was occupied by German soldiers. On one of the neighbouring farms, also German occupied, they were shooting grenades towards Nijmegen where the Allies were. That's probably 25 miles away. Grenades were real humdingers, like bombs. If they exploded they would leave a hole five feet deep and about eight feet across. We had our German shepherd with us one time. He had been used with a dog cart to take the milk cans to the roadside. All of a sudden the Germans started to fire these grenades, and we knew there would be a response from the Allies. We were in the orchard, with a fence around it. Then the answer came, a high-pitched whine of a grenade coming in. There was a fence around the orchard, about five feet high. I jumped over the fence to get out of the way and into the ditch behind it. I lay there face-up because there was water in it. The nearest grenade fell maybe ten feet away, and the pieces of hot shrapnel landed right next to me. And they were hot! I tried to jump that high fence again some time later, and couldn't do it.

After the noise stopped, Dad and I tried to get home. We came by a bomb shelter, when another grenade was launched. We jumped into it and there were already

German soldiers in it. They had been in a septic pit and boy, didn't that stink. We didn't stay very long. They didn't attack us; they were as scared as we were. Anyway, we got home. That is one of the days I really remember well.

We had to be evacuated again and we went to a great-uncle at Dieren, on the other side of Velp. There were always German soldiers on the loose who had become separated from their regiments and they would go to farms and demand stuff, or just take it. We strung a rope between the main farmhouse building and a barn, and if the door was pulled open on the barn it would rattle something in the farmhouse that would wake everybody up. My Dad and the great-uncle and his two sons took turns staying up at night to make sure nothing would happen.

One particular night the rattle came on. We all jumped up. My great-uncle, Dad, and the two sons all had pitchforks and I had an axe because I was the smallest. We all went to the milk barn and there were three soldiers there. They wanted a young heifer. I remember the three soldiers stood with their backs to each other to make a triangle, and we went around them with our pitchforks and an axe. They had their guns out, but aiming up in the air. I imagine it is very uncomfortable to be surrounded by people with pitchforks, just circling you. So they left. They went to the next farm, we heard that the next day, and they shot through the door and stole three cows there.

Another thing I remember are the V1 or V2 rockets, and one morning one of them went off. The guys were milking and my great-uncle was in the kitchen. A rocket went by and the whole house vibrated. It landed about 600 feet away from the farm. I remember seeing the hole later, and our house would have fit into it. The windows all blew in. My great-uncle was bald and the pieces hit his head. His whole head was bleeding. That must have been in March. We were sleeping on the floor, and I can still see the window bulging in. My little brother and I pulled the blankets over our head, and when the window blew, the blankets were covered in glass.

We went there in November and we stayed there until we were freed on the 16th of April. When we came home there were no doors and no windows. There were land mines all around the village, and a lot of the doors were booby-trapped. One person I knew quite well got hit by that, and his hand was always shaking. Anyone who got home had to be very careful opening doors.

We found ammunition lying around, and we gathered it up and threw it in a ditch and buried it. All the land mines and other ammunition around the village were gathered up, some of it really big, for panzer, armoured cars. One big pile was by the roadside. On the first weekend of May another family had just come home too. There was the father and the mother, and two daughters with young boyfriends. Nobody has ever found out what happened, but apparently they went by one of those piles of land mines, and the whole family was gone. They were blown up.

I find fall difficult because that's when it all happened. Fall weather brings it all back.

The Allied soldiers were lost

Harry Caubo

One of the most memorable days in my life was September 17, 1944. The 119th Regiment and the 2nd Armored Division (the 'Old Hickory Division') liberated my old hometown of Heerlen, Limburg. They fought the German 81st Army corps, commanded by General Friedrich August Schack. We had no school as winter came on, since all local schools were used by the US Forces. What I really loved to do during my teen years was go to Terworm, a forest where I could roam around and enjoy nature. It was across from my boyhood home. It was cold and snowy.

Suddenly I spotted an American patrol approaching in the distance. They stopped close to where I was. It was an open jeep with the commander and two lieutenants. I saw a couple of tanks and a couple of trucks with some very cold G.I.'s. In the lead jeep they were studying a map. Everyone was very interested and looking at that map. And that included me. I could hear from their conversation that they were lost. I was well-versed in the English language, having taken English for several years in school. They did not know what their location was. They kept looking for Germany on the map. It was an understandable error, as the German border was only eight miles away. I told them to flip the map over and I showed them where they were: near Heerlen in Holland.

One of the lieutenants whispered: "Don't trust that damn 'Kraut'... he may be sending us the wrong way".

It took me a while to convince them that I was 'one of them'. I pointed at the map again. Finally a big grin appeared on their faces. They believed me and gave me a couple of packs of chewing gum and some chocolate. This was a treasure during the tail end of the war in 1944. They started up their jeep and the trucks. The tank engines were fired up and with a wave of their arms the Americans disappeared in the snow and fog. I never saw them again.

And this was my contribution to WW II.

We lived in a cigar factory

Joe Verstappen

I was a kid, fourteen years old, and was in a big field on Sunday, September 17, 1944 with a couple of my friends. We were going to explode some ammo and a hand grenade stolen from the Germans. They had been moving towards Die Heimat, their home country. In the early afternoon the planes came, and hundreds of paratroopers jumped into that field near Eerde, where we were going to explode our German loot. When the paratroopers dropped all around us, we forgot in a hurry about exploding hand grenades or ammo. We were so happy our liberators had come, and the 17th of September was one of the happiest days of my life.

In the southeast region of the Netherlands we got liberated early, and didn't have to go through that terrible hunger winter as the rest of Holland did. We were spared that, but suffered our homes to be destroyed or burned or partly damaged, like our home in Noord Brabant which took shells from both sides, the Germans and the Allies. We had to evacuate our home and live in a cigar factory in Sint-Oedenrode. We also lived in brick ovens, and it took several weeks before we could get back to our badly damaged home. I remember we moved back in, and the ceiling was like a sieve, full of holes from the shells. In the morning we were wet. The first thing we had to do was fix the roof. Most of the stuff in the house was stolen. The English had two cannons in our garden and they lived in the house when we came back home.

That winter was very cold, and fuel was scarce. We lived in the country and didn't starve like other regions of the country. I remember we had a pig, and it was slaughtered for food. Some of our neighbours were burned out, and a lot of them ended up living in their chicken coops.

The sirens started to howl

Josine Eikelenboom

We had a summer cottage at Epe, northeast of Apeldoorn in the province of Gelderland. When we went there, Dad remained in Rotterdam for his work but visited us on weekends. In December we moved to Arnhem, a paradise after Rotterdam. We had a large house and garden, with a park at the end of the street. We children hardly noticed the war, except that my little Jewish friend had suddenly disappeared…

Then came that Sunday, September 17, 1944. My brother and I were in Sunday School when the sirens started to howl at 11.00 a.m. We heard airplanes and the sounds of shots far away, but there was no 'safe' signal at the end. Parents came to get their children until there were only five left. Mrs. Kijlstra, our teacher, decided to deliver us to our homes. The streets were quiet then and we got home safely, although we could hear something from the direction of Oosterbeek and Heelsum. That afternoon we heard planes again and my father sent us into the cellar. He stayed outdoors to see what was going on, and shouted down to us about the spectacular aerial display as the sky filled with gliders pulled by transport planes. We saw countless dots emerging from those planes, paratroopers who would land on the heath at Heelsum. They were meant to ensure access to the Rhine bridge at Nijmegen. Some planes were hit by anti-aircraft fire and plunged, burning, to the ground. I remember retreating, shocked, into the cellar.

During the battle for Arnhem, the food supply stagnated and there was no more water. We filled buckets from the ponds at Sonsbeek, a large park with historic homes on the edge of Arnhem. Of course the ongoing battle made living conditions untenable for the civilian population, and after five days we were ordered to evacuate the town. We headed for Heerde, where my grandparents, and an aunt and an uncle lived. Father loaded up his bicycle, pulling our old baby carriage behind it. This contained important documents, the family silver, and essential clothing. Mother carried her youngest son on the back of her bike, and our children's bikes were loaded with blankets and coats. We were allowed one or two things of our own and I took some books. They fell off the bike into the mud as we rode along; I still have them, stains and all.

Before we left, Father had buried our antique Frisian clock and his most beloved books in the garden, while Mother wanted to leave everything behind in good order so she scrubbed the breakfast table before our departure. When we returned the following June, half the roof had been blown off, German soldiers had partied in the house and had dumped pots of jam into the piano. The buried property lay thrown around the garden.

In the days of the Arnhem evacuation, the roads to Ede and Apeldoorn were filled with people pulling carts and baby carriages filled with goods, or riding heavily loaded bicycles which they hoped to bring to safety. One or two trucks, or horse-drawn wagons, transported entire families. Even German army trucks passed us, carrying captured Tommies. Those boys with their red berets were passionately cheered by the evacuees as they came by.

Unfortunately, we would have to wait more than half a year before we were actually liberated.

The fighting in Blerick-Venlo

From the diary of John Holthuis

Sunday, September 3, 1944

Since Friday, column after column of Germans has been passing by on Antonius Street. Bicycles were confiscated, as well as other transportation. Even horses and carriages were taken out of farmers' barns. Accompanying the retreating Germans were Belgian families, including girls who feared having their heads shaved. Sunday at 6.00 p.m., dozens of planes attacked the airfield. All the anti-aircraft guns in Blerick and Venlo shot into the air. One bomber was hit but got away. Sadly, some bombs fell on Herunger Street and took the lives of eleven people.

Monday, September 4

The airfield seems to have sustained major damage. On the town square, all the young men are grouped together, guarded by Nazi sympathizers. Anyone coming out of the eight streets to the square is nabbed and added to the group; no excuses. Railway workers are also summoned. Anyone trying to run away is shot. That happened to A. Valks in Venlo, who was shot to death. The entire group of men had to fill the holes in the airfield and clean up the runways. When the air raid sirens went off, many young men ran away.

The columns of soldiers on Antonius Street continue to pass by. All the soldiers walk around with a notice from

General Model acknowledging that England has won this battle, but that England will lose the war. Soldiers are ordered to report to their divisions, take no plunder, not set off unnecessary ammunition, and to keep their heads up and shoulders straight so that 'the enemy will see no soldiers who appear defeated. The Fuhrer needs time to produce his new weapons in sufficient numbers for the battle to continue'. It's a sure sign that the end of the war is near. The Allies have already arrived in southern Limburg and Eindhoven.

Tuesday, September 5

The British are in Thorn and the Americans have made it to Breda. The Germans hear the news and their withdrawal surges. The town of Blerick anticipates its liberation, since the Allies have already reached Maasniel. The people in hiding return to the streets, knowing that the Germans are withdrawing, and the collaborators are gone.

Thursday, September 7

A whole group of collaborators have returned. Their last-ditch actions create an even greater hatred for them. Here they grab a bag of flour, there a bag of something else. Everything that catches their eye is taken away: bikes, motor bikes, cars. Locked doors are broken down, and anything hidden is hauled away.

Friday, September 8

The Germans have chosen Blerick as a site for taking a stand against the Allies. They have placed four cannons by the bridge and some near De Staai. Another seven are on the Venlo side of the harbour under the bridge.

These cannons apparently can shoot at airplanes. During the night there is constant shooting at planes passing overhead. The failure of the Allies to appear is felt by everyone.

Sunday, September 10
We were awakened at 5:30 by the sound of heavy shooting aimed at planes overhead. When it stopped we decided to attend the early Mass. Ten minutes later we had to get home as the Germans were planning a raid. In the evening many young men took off under cover of darkness.

Monday, September 11
161 men have gone to work for the Germans. To improve the view for the Germans, all the shrubbery was cut down, even weeping willows and other trees in the park. Many houses on Railway Street had to be evacuated, and part of Antonius Street.

Tuesday, September 12
About 4000 Germans, Polish, Russian and Belgian women have come to dig the tank trench, since Blerick people have refused to do it. The entire row of houses beside the bridge was blown up. The NAD and the Halmans building exploded, and Van Steegh's garage.

Wednesday, September 13
The Germans in charge of the work crews entered the houses to find and confiscate any remaining bicycles. The remaining houses by the bridge were dynamited. It happened so quickly that the Ewals had no time to remove the contents. Until 10.00 p.m. the windows

rattled from the explosions. Apparently the airfield needs to be totally destroyed. Since Friday we have seen no German planes, but many Allied planes.

Thursday, September 14

The Germans want the tank trench to be finished as quickly as possible. Even girls walking through the streets are put to work on it. This evening the large bunker was blown to smithereens. Another order was posted commanding men between 14 and 60 to show up tomorrow morning. If they do not obey, then women aged 16 to 45 will be picked up to dig the trench and clean up rubble by the bridge and airfield. It is forbidden to leave the area.

Friday, September 15

Hurrah! The German broadcast announced that they had lost the city of Maastricht. The Green Police were here this afternoon but found nothing. The explosions on the air field continued all day.

Saturday, September 16

Despite German threats, girls and women were not picked up. This evening bulletins were posted stating that not nearly enough Blerick men had shown up. From now on any man who does not show up, or tries to leave, will be shot as soon as he is found. Work hours will be from 7.00 a.m. to 6.00 p.m.

Sunday, September 17

Sunday morning most of the men from Blerick and Venlo gathered by the bridge. By 9.00 a.m. we were still standing there. When we finally arrived at the trench site we were accused by an officer with a big mouth of being late. After that tirade we were divided into two groups. The ones with their own shovels had to go to the left side and the others to the right. At 10.00 a.m. a wagon arrived with shovels and we were put to work. We have to dig a trench three and a twelve feet deep. Very little work was done, just some sand dug here and tossed there. After an hour of doing basically nothing, we heard planes coming. We counted more than two hundred, followed by fighter planes. Everyone left the trench and hurried home. We took our shovels with us and kept a good lookout for soldiers. We don't plan to return.

Monday, September 18

Allied planes flew from morning till night. We heard that paratroopers have landed in Eindhoven, Nijmegen, and Tilburg. We no longer have gas or electricity.

Tuesday, September 19

Eindhoven is in the hands of the Allies. It was a day of planes constantly overhead. At 4.30 a.m. the lights suddenly came back on.

Wednesday, September 20

The electricity we always got from the mines in southern Limburg now comes from the electrical plant in Venlo. Smaller towns still have to do without. The mines are under British control, and they stopped the power transmission from there.

This afternoon some Luftwaffe soldiers came by to confiscate bicycles and pigs. All they got on the entire street was one bike. Now that there is no longer any strict control, most people no longer go to work. We can tell that the Allies are coming closer because all day we hear the thunder of cannons and see Allied reconnaissance planes overhead.

Thursday, September 21

On the city square there were 500 Germans, more than half of them injured and handicapped. They left this evening, except for a small group to guard the supplies and ammunition.

Most of them are anti-Hitler, and it was only two weeks ago that they were forced to leave their homes and families. They tell us they have no idea how to use a gun or toss a grenade.

Friday, September 22

The withdrawal of the Germans has been postponed for another day. This afternoon, Luftwaffe soldiers confiscated the wagon belonging to Van Schrobbers. At the assembly area, wagons and tracked vehicles are being unloaded.

The area is guarded by lightweight defense cannons. All afternoon they shot at low flying planes and at fighter planes.

Saturday, September 23

There are once again many planes in the air and the Germans try to shoot them down without success. Last night we sat in the cellar for half an hour because there were more planes than we have seen or heard all this time. Tons of phosphorus were dropped into Germany. We could see that the resulting fires looked like an inferno.

Tuesday, September 26

Everywhere you can see people strengthening their air raid shelters. We put up a wall of bricks with a layer of sand in front of them, plus an iron plate two or three inches thick. Altogether this wall is now three feet thick.

Another notice was posted this evening: The number of men showing up to dig the trench was so minimal that it is considered an act of sabotage. On Wednesday at exactly 7.00 a.m. all males from 16 to 60 have to show up at the market square and will be taken to the job site. If this is not adhered to, Venlo citizens will be shot publicly. In addition, 2,000 young men will be shipped to Germany. Those who show up will be paid three guilders per day. The warning is so threatening that many men decide to go to work.

Wednesday, September 27

At 6.45 a.m. we gathered by the bridge. It was cold. Led by a guard we crossed the bridge. They do not trust us, as is the case with every Dutch person they encounter. That actually raised some pride in us. Once we arrived at the square we were grouped in rows of three by our own traitorous citizens. Armed with machine guns they shouted and yelled at us. None of us dared open our mouths.

After it had been established that there were enough of us, we were herded to the airfield. There we were put to work, but very little real work was done. We looked up at the planes and told jokes. At 5.00 p.m. we could return home.

Later we learned that we had been 'bad', and as punishment we had to carry two shovels and two axes. We also did not receive our pay. Another bulletin posted carried a strong reminder that all the German-imposed conditions remained in effect.

Thursday, September 28

Yesterday the train station was hit with rocket projectiles shot off by Typhoon planes. We saw it happen above our heads.

Friday, September 30

Another bulletin from the Mayor, and the Germans announced that on Sunday morning at eight, all the labourers are to be on the job again. Resistance would mean punishment as outlined previously. Only 300 men showed up, one-seventh of the number on Wednesday.

Tuesday, October 3

Yesterday's bulletin netted fewer than forty men. How sad for the Germans, as they had expected such enthusiastic cooperation for their trench digging project. As could be expected, the result was another raid with a few more victims.

Wednesday, October 4

Raids are being carried out everywhere. Because of the poor showing of workers twelve leading citizens have been arrested and are being held hostage, including a doctor, the town administrator, several rectors, and a lawyer.

Saturday, October 7

We were warned this evening that very likely a very vicious raid will take place tomorrow. A decision is made not to go to church the next morning.

Sunday, October 8

Father, who has been in hiding elsewhere decided, in spite of the warning, to attend church at 8.00 a.m. This resulted in problems. At the end of the Mass, the men headed for the church exit only to be faced by German soldiers. Quickly they headed to the side exits, but there were soldiers there as well. Some of the men were nabbed. Dr. Vallen told Dad to accompany him since, as a doctor, nothing much would happen to him. Dad said he preferred to stay in church. Dr. Vallen left church and was immediately picked up, despite his protests. Once the way was clear, the others vanished in many creative ways. Later in the day we heard that the same had happened in neighbouring towns. The men who had been picked up were loaded on trucks and taken to Germany. Many of those who had been in hiding were thus still picked up. In Maasbree, some two hundred were grabbed.

Afterwards, bulletins appeared with the words, 'This town has been politically and militarily cleansed'. No men were allowed to appear in public without a special permit. Without the permit they would be shot.

If you do not want to be transported to Germany, you spend night and day in small holes. At night we can no longer stand it because it is impossible to get any sleep. So we sleep in our own beds. About 400 Germans have arrived in Venlo.

On Thursday a raid was held on Nieuwborg street. Suddenly a child with German parents piped up: "You should take a look in the factory." A German soldier leaped over the factory's fence and found Vermeersen's son who had not been able to get away quickly enough. The soldier shot at him to make him come down from some scaffolding. A troop of Germans surrounded the factory, but when they entered they found no one. Now and then they were so close to the hiding places that those inside shook in their boots.

On Friday morning, a convoy of planes bombed the bridge. Half the bombs fell on the city. One half of Nassau Street is completely demolished, also the Rembrandt theatre, Titulaar's shoe store, Ratskeller, the clinic, a section of Kleef Street, and a German guard post. Dr. Van Rooy, just released the day before, was outside close to where the bombing was going on. The air pressure of the bombing tore apart his lungs and he died. The number of deaths has already risen to more than forty. The British air force will likely return because not all the anti-aircraft installations on the bridge have been destroyed yet.

Monday, October 16

The droning of many planes woke us. Slowly, ignoring the anti-aircraft shells coming our way, we saw the planes head to Germany. We counted 24, but then more and more groups of 24 or 35 follow until we lost count. They are accompanied by many fighter planes. Since they fly higher than the other planes, they show up as beautiful silhouettes against the bright blue sky, with exhaust streams coming out of the rear.

The list of casualties and missing persons from the bombings of October 13 and 15 has now been reported: thirty-five people.

Too hot to handle

Henry Niezen

In November 1944, the Canadians, Scots and Poles were south along the Maas River. Our family had to take in a German *'wachtmeister'*, a sergeant-major with the artillery. He came on a motorbike stolen in Walcheren. His name was Heinrich Lopeter. He had been looking after some field guns and 'ack ack' (anti-aircraft guns). The Germans had set these up under a row of poplar trees along inundated land. After they had fired on some Spitfires, damaging some, a spotter plane came. At night they moved to a different spot. Next morning all hell broke loose when the Typhoons came. Their rockets set a farmhouse on fire. People came to help, but a cache of artillery shells, stored in the stable attached to the back of the house, exploded. It killed nine civilians and a German soldier whom I saw dying in the arms of a Green Cross nurse.

When I saw the planes firing I grabbed my grandmother and put her on the floor in a corner, between two brick walls in the back of the house. Ceiling tile came down, the front gable was split, the yard was covered with big chunks of clay. The dust from the thatched roof covered everything. I was surprised to see how a piece of shrapnel can gouge a hole into a brick wall. The family pitched in to clean up. A carpenter came to put the tiles back on the ceiling, and before dark we were ready to sleep in our own beds.

Shortly afterwards the *wachtmeister* came with a hind leg of lamb, but grandmother would not take it. When he explained where he had bought the meat she relented. Maybe Heinrich was sorry he got us into such a mess. Whenever a marauding soldier came around I would only have to say, "I'll call the *wachtmeister*", and they would beat a hasty retreat.

Later that year we got the V1 buzz bombs flying over. Some would malfunction and fly around and around until they hit something. I saw one red hot one explode in the air; lucky that it didn't come down. We had the front windows blown out twice in one week. We had lots of glass from the cold frames under which we grew strawberries. Now they were stacked up with planks and sod on top against the shrapnel that was raining down from the 88s firing at the Waal River bridge.

On one overcast morning a formation of heavy bombers came. I heard a whine and bit the dust. A chunk of shrapnel fell close to me. I picked it up and burned my fingers. Lesson learned: never pick up anything too hot too handle.

Refugees in the Arnhem suburb of Velp

From the diary of Jan van Hensbergen

Note from Wilbert Stroeve: I received a copy of a journal kept by one of my parents' friends, Jan van Hensbergen. It started on the 14th of September 1944, a few days before the first Allied attempts to cross the Rhine River in the area of Arnhem. Jan van Hensbergen lived and worked as an accountant in Velp, a suburb of Arnhem and was a member of the Dutch Resistance.

Thursday, September 14, 1944

An alarming telephone conversation with Mr. Visser from the bank. All companies are to shut down their operations. So I withdrew the entire balance from our accounts and I recommended that others, including Ton, do the same. Tomorrow morning at 06.45 all staff are to be drafted into the German armed forces. Everyone is very dejected by this. As a precautionary measure, we paid advances to all our staff. We agreed with them that after the war they could return to their jobs. We all shook hands and wished each other well. A lot of stuff was stored away so that it wouldn't be readily found. The personnel archives are safe.

Friday, September 15

First day at home. Made preparations for going underground to avoid contact with the Germans, should they come and search the house. The announcements on Thursday now conflict with the rules of the authorities: able-bodied men who are out of work are to report to the authorities, presumably so they can be sent to Germany to work in the factories there. I gave Mijnie instructions on how to forward future communications in code. At 5 o'clock I went to Miepie in order to spend the remainder of the war in hiding.

Saturday, September 16

Nothing in particular. Mijnie visited me in the evening and during the night. It has been four weeks since we slept together.

Sunday, September 17

I was awakened at 9.00 a.m. by the air raid sirens. At 11.00 we heard the third air raid siren. The first bombs fell on the city. This was the first time that I actually saw bombs fall. A huge column of smoke rose from the center of the city. The attack by twin-tailed aircraft was against the German barracks. There was heavy German anti-aircraft fire. I did not see any Tommies come down. There were many English fighter planes involved. The electricity went out and the water supply was shut down. At 1.05 p.m. the 'all clear' siren was given. Electricity and water is restored. At 1.15 the air raid sirens sounded again. Groups of six bombers each right above our heads dropped their bombs (due to the speed of the planes themselves, the bombs would still strike the ground some distance away). The bombs fell with huge explosions, perhaps in the area of Oosterbeek? That is the rail line from Nijmegen to Arnhem. German anti-aircraft fire was noticeably missing. All of us were huddled together in the hallway, underneath the staircase. Mama Miep was very nervous and concerned. A couple of times I got up and went to the balcony to see what was going on, and to try to assess the damage that was being inflicted.

Freight gliders had landed somewhere between Oosterbeek and Ede. There were on-going fighter activities above the airfield at Deelen. As far as we could tell, not a single English fighter was shot down. The reports came in around 6.00 p.m. The Tommies have taken over Oosterbeek! The Germans are starting to set up defenses at Schelmse Road and Amsterdam Road. All kinds of material is falling from the sky: half a roof, a tree, pieces of cardboard. Around 7 o'clock we hear the first machine-gun fire from Arnhem. There is a huge fire in the centre of the city. During the night there is a fantastic spectacle, the explosions of munitions in the Willem barracks. Around 10 o'clock a new fire developed in the direction of Velp. We sat around by candlelight. Around midnight we went to bed still dressed. No light, no gas, no water. We are all suffering from lack of news and emotional stress. We know that liberation is at hand. The orders from the police are: 'windows and doors open, the bunkers are being blown up'. The entire night we constantly heard explosions.

Monday, September 18

We are starting to get used to the rifle and grenade fire. Around 10 o'clock the first refugees from Arnhem appear, heading for Hoogkamp. According to one of them half of Velp is flattened. First we ate with Miep and then we walked to Velp. Got home around 4.00 p.m. Frieda en Ton came down to our floor because it was too dangerous above. We decided to stay together. In Velp the 'Krauts' set fire to Naeff. (Naeff was a restaurant used as the local German headquarters).

Tuesday, September 19

As we do every day, we got water from the farmer next door. Much activity on the street. 'The Hague, Amsterdam, Rotterdam, Gouda, and Delft are liberated. 900 landing craft between Katwijk and Hoek van Holland in the invasion. Cologne has been taken'. These were the reports that everybody believed but which turned out to be false.

Around 4.30 the paratroopers were thrown out of Oosterbeek. We were able to confirm this from the roof. Three freight gliders crashed while in flames. Two parachutes did not open. Wolfje (Ton & Frieda's German shepherd) was run over by a 'Kraut' car. The first prisoners of war passed by before us.

Thursday, September 21

More English POWs. About a thousand of them have passed by here. Again paratroopers, not that many, in the direction of Oosterbeek.

Friday, September 22

The fire in Arnhem is extinguished. We still hear a lot of noise from the direction of Nijmegen. The main force is there. The center of Arnhem is completely devoid of people. There are reports that all of Arnhem is to be evacuated.

Saturday, September 23

Large groups of refugees are coming out of Arnhem, a

very depressing sight. A woman with bare feet passes by. Frieda gives her a pair of shoes. Fenny and Luc also arrive with fourteen others and are now downstairs in de Rooy's small room. I got some hay for them to lie on. They do not want to be upstairs.

Again paratroopers are dropped in the direction of Oosterbeek. The number of POWs that has passed by, is now around 1,500.

Sunday, September 24

Supposedly before 8.00 p.m., all of Arnhem should be evacuated. I helped Mr. van Asselt by moving his parents' goods using a carrier tricycle. (Carrier tricycles were used in those days to transport small amounts of goods. It's like a small single-axle wagon with two wheels replacing the front wheel of a standard bicycle).

A very depressing sight coming from Arnhem, everyone with white flags. It is claimed that columns of refugees heading for Apeldoorn were shot at. Schut with his wife, and both their parents, also take up residence downstairs.

Today I had two drinks at van Asselt's and we ate stew there.

Monday, September 25

Velp looks like a major city of the world, with so many people that it makes you think of being on Broadway. We ate chicken. I saw three English fighters (or perhaps they were German) crash. Large bombs were dropped near the hospital in Sonsbeek. We sat for 15 minutes in the bomb shelter. (Chicken was suddenly readily available because due to the bombing attacks the cold storage facilities in Arnhem had been put out of commission and all the frozen meats there had to be distributed, lest they spoil).

Tuesday, September 26
The English have arrived in Elst. Great optimism.

Wednesday, September 27
Schut's father was killed by a bomb when he was returning a carrier tricycle to De Steeg (an area between Velp and Dieren).

The destruction of Liessel

Martha Gubbels

We lived in Liessel, North Brabant. We were liberated for the first time on September 23, 1944. I remember the fighting did not seem too heavy somehow. The soldiers came into town in big tanks, handing out chocolates and crackers to the children, cigarettes to the adults. The Germans had retreated to a swampy area, De Peel, strengthening their forces. For weeks they shot missiles into the town, damaging the local Catholic church and other places, wounding some people, killing others. In the last days of October they were back in full force. We had to pack up and leave our home and go to Asten, in the southeast of the province, where it was safe. My Dad said we were lucky, being all together and okay.

I remember a family of eighteen who were trying to leave their home, and three of the children were killed, some were wounded. I believe the German military doctor looked after them.

Fighting became heavy in our area, with American and British soldiers fighting against the Germans. One of my cousins who stayed behind in Liessel with neighbours, said at times the whole town looked like it was on fire. Two-thirds of the town and the surrounding area were destroyed.

Our area was eventually liberated by Scottish soldiers who fought one to one with the Germans, and were backed up by British tanks. Many, many died. It was been said that the fighting in the Liessel area was the worst since Normandy.

I lost three cousins in the war. One was a policeman who was transporting English-speaking men, believed to be pilots. They were stopped by German officers and my cousin was shot when these men spoke. Another cousin was sent to a concentration camp in Germany. He returned alive in 1945, telling his mother that the hunger was the worst. He died of malnutrition shortly afterwards in Groningen. His sister died in a car accident during Liberation festivities in Helmond, where she was working.

My family returned without me and three of my siblings, to find that everything was destroyed by fire. I was sent to Helmond to live with an aunt and uncle for nine months. The other three lived with another aunt and uncle in Westerhoven for six months. Later we found that many people had worked with the Resistance and saved lives of people of different nationalities. But some were not so lucky and were killed by the Germans and the NSB, the Dutch traitors.

I returned to Liessel in 1992 for a visit and went to the unveiling of a monument in honour of the liberators and the local people who died. Two of my cousins' names are on this monument.

Children's home 'Gelria'

From the diary of Clasina Wisman

Clasina Elizabeth Wisman was the director of a children's home in the town of Berg en Dal, about 14 miles from Arnhem. In her journal she related events connected to the children, staff, various battles, and her efforts to feed some of the Allied soldiers who had dropped from the sky.

The name of the children's home was 'Gelria', and it consisted of three houses side by side that dated back to the 1920s. Not all the children were orphans.There were sixty of them at the time Market Garden got underway, ranging in age from infants to older girls. Boys were normally accepted only up to the age of ten, but the war situation prevented a few from leaving at that age. Some were sent by the youth court system or Social Services, suggesting less than optimal backgrounds. Others had parents who retained contact with their children, suggesting that war conditions may have been responsible for them being cared for at Gelria. In one case (in April 1945) Clasina notes that a baby had come in whose mother had been hospitalized while the father was away all day.

Clasina's journal begins on September 3, 1944, as German troops and Dutch traitors were fleeing in wild disorder towards the German border, while Allied forces intent on liberating Holland approached from the south.

Sunday, September 3

News is coming in that the hour of liberation is coming near.

Monday, September 4

Went to Nijmegen to discuss with school board members whether it's safe to send the children to school under these conditions. Both said they would prefer not to take the responsibility. The retreat of the German forces is in full swing. This morning I was told not to allow any leave for our staff, and anyone not here is to be called back. Sent urgent telegrams to Leid and Corrie to return if possible. Columns of soldiers have been crossing the German border from here, dragging along anything they can obtain.

Tuesday, September 5

The news is becoming more and more enthusiastic. Many planes in the sky, and there's much shooting so that the house shakes at times. Trains seem to have stopped, but mail is still coming through; telephone connections to Utrecht and Apeldoorn are out. At 6:30 tonight, big excitement: Corrie arrived. She walked all the way from Den Bosch, in the middle of retreating troops, nine hours on the road. An hour later, Leid also arrived, happy to be back, and all staff is now on duty. Heavy droning through the night.

Wednesday, September 6

Schools are officially closed. All the N.S.B. (Dutch traitors) have left town. We're going to order a flagpole, and already have a good flag on hand. Was able to buy orange ribbon for all the girls, so we're ready for liberation!

Thursday, September 7

The mood is a bit depressed, perhaps not right but

understandable. No mail getting through, and news on food supplies is not rosy. We're getting far less milk now, and have to go to the farmer for more. We hear that our bread rations will be halved. It seems as though the hardest time is about to come.

Tuesday, September 12

On Saturday we heard that there will be billeting of soldiers in private homes. Until now we're still clear of that, but there are army trucks in our lane, guarded by sentries. I allow no one to go out except for the girls going for milk in the evening.

Since we'll have to be careful with the food supply we've begun preserving tomatoes, carrots, peas, applesauce, and blackberries, as our little ones will need food this winter. The children are gathering beech nuts which we'll roast and grind up for nut butter. Guus Schenk is an irreplaceable help to us, as she is unbelievably handy with a needle. The assistants also are helping to repair and alter any clothing we've been given. From unusable old coats they've made warm hats for all the children. Who's to say there will be goods available once we're free?

Thursday, September 14

I've been able to buy ten winter coats for the children, and will hear tomorrow how many dresses will be available. The girls are delighted, of course. During the day we see city people coming through, looking for potatoes, with the strangest vehicles and carts. The city of Nijmegen seems empty. No man or student dares appear in public, everything and everyone being requisitioned by the Wehrmacht.

Friday, September 15

Maastricht has fallen to the Allies. We're impatient and would like to see this liberation going faster, especially in the cities where food is in short supply.

Sunday, September 17

Since six this evening we've had no more German troops in our lane.

Americans! In church this morning we had trouble understanding the minister, with all the droning and bombing going on. He quickly finished up and we got home. Then the noise really broke loose. Great formations of bombers, covered by fighter planes, hundreds of parachutes being dropped. Apart from the noise and the danger it was an interesting spectacle to watch. The afternoon was a bit quieter, but just before six Dries, our gardener, came to tell us there were Tommies coming through. And yes, there were the paratroopers. They were tired and sweaty and sat down in the lane. They asked for water and although our supply is shut off, we gave them fresh rain water. We also had a nice pear for each one of them.

Mr. Fisscher told us he already had the first Camel cigarette and that fifty Americans had captured the large villa which housed Germans until this morning. We had to tell them when the Germans left, and whether they might still be close to here.

We quickly made a very large pan of tomato soup for the soldiers, and in thanks they gave us an entire parachute that we can cut up into kerchiefs for all the girls. Also cigarettes, chocolate and so on. They are well supplied. They warned us to make sure no light was visible tonight, since the Germans may still try something tonight. In each of our houses we have assistants standing watch in turn, and of course I will stay up. The girls went to bed with their clothes on and all is ready to grab if necessary. Luckily the power and water came back on at 8.00 p.m., making us think the Germans must be out of Nijmegen.

It's hard to realize we're actually free already, but of course we don't know how things will go tomorrow. The mood here has been jubilant and it was hard to control the girls. I saw that a few of them had managed to grab and hide a cigarette. When it was bedtime I said to them, "Just go to the bathroom now to smoke your cigarettes." They couldn't believe their ears, but they were so delighted they went to bed like lambs. I hope I haven't done something wrong here, but it really wasn't easy to keep the lid on.

I will never forget 6.00 p.m., September 17!

Monday, September 18

We're entering the second day of our liberation. This morning early our American guests came to our rain barrel to wash, shave, and brush their teeth. The tomato soup seems to have pleased them as they mentioned it, so we cooked up another big panful. The soldiers are waiting to meet up with troops coming from Brabant, but the latter are not hurrying here yet. There was much action in the sky this afternoon and we saw dozens of gliders, with a bomber circling protectively above them. We're cut off from the world at present.

The whole town is decorated with orange and everyone is friendly with the Yankees. The guys don't like to be mistaken for Tommies (British) who they consider a bit slow, leaving them, the Yanks, to do the hard work.

I have to say again that these men are enormously well supplied, with complete shaving kit, Lux and Lysol soap, a small leather sewing kit, and numerous food ingredients. They're generously doling out their supplies. They're not getting any hot meals, however, which explains their fondness for our soup. We see them slinking through the woods with their guns at the ready, the way we used to see it on film. And now we're in the middle of it with sixty children.

It seems that the children are getting used to it, and the calmer we are, the better for them. No power or water this afternoon; hopefully it will come back tonight, especially as we have to do all the laundry on site now. Luckily the baker was able to bake, and we were able to get groceries on our ration cards.

10.00 p.m. This evening there was some hard fighting here at Berg en Dal, also at Beek and Nijmegen. Alcha's house burned down, and at Hamer and Koot all the windows are smashed. The Germans were in the back of the Mission House and the Americans in the front. They have partial control of Nijmegen, but no bridges yet.

I have fifteen refugees here, two families plus another family just for the night. An American just came in, asking for the lady who speaks English. He took me aside and I worried that we would be told to evacuate. However, he just asked if I knew anyone who could provide food for four persons once or twice. It involved a small advance group which had to move on as quickly as possible. I offered him a couple of loaves of bread, and gave him a quick plate of soup. He said he had been part of the landing in France, and that Holland was so much neater and tidier than France or Belgium. You have to admire these men, so calm and self-assured.

They are still waiting for reinforcements, so they've had to clear this area with very few men. According to Mr. Fisscher, they fought like lions.

Tuesday, September 19

Yesterday when we finally got everything organized and even found beds for the refugee women, and were ready to tuck in ourselves, there was a knock on the kitchen door. Five or six army staff came in, wanting to study their maps. By the light of our lantern they conferred for twenty minutes with worried, tight-lipped faces. They have wonderful maps, with every house and footpath on them. There was severe fighting overnight but by morning things had calmed down.

Van Schaik was unable to milk his cows last night but they were at it this morning when we came along, so we got it fresh from the cow. After breakfast I went for bread and met Mr Leenders, who's the acting mayor now. He asked if I could manage with the current food supply, and said he'd much appreciate us feeding the soldiers hot meals. He will see that I get enough potatoes. Using his name, I was able to get sufficient groceries at the store, including 25 packs of butter. The grocer is no longer sleeping in his house, which is on the main route, but came from his bomb shelter long enough to serve me. The baker has to do everything by hand, without electricity, and was two hours behind. Hopefully it will be quiet enough to go fetch the bread.

Noon. Mr. Fisscher called, saying the first American tanks are in Nijmegen, and the British army is at the Graafse Bridge. That's a relief, especially for the Americans here. I passed on the news to Dr. Roessingh at Beek, where they haven't seen any Americans yet but are hiding in the cellar under loud bangs. He wondered if I couldn't send them an American with a loaf of bread! Apparently Nijmegen is burning, including the Protestant Hospital.

Latest news: Nijmegen is being cleared, fleeing Germans are coming this way and are under fire, so that the noise is deafening here. The Resistance is active also, walking around with orange bands on their arms, some of them with cartridge belts around their civilian outfits.

6.00 p.m. The Big Hotel is back in the hands of the owner, who is distributing all kinds of stuff to the population. Carts full have been brought here, all free: big bags of pears, crates of jam, honey, coffee, and to help us cook for the soldiers, a large crate of ready to serve soup, rice, a big pan of gravy with some meat in it, pork chops, cucumbers, and boiled potatoes. Received five liters of milk tonight so that our littlest ones won't go short. The older ones can eat pears. It's amazing how well we eat each day. The baker is still baking for us, and I had staff harvest endive, beets and cabbage from the garden when the sky was peaceful for a bit.

8.00 p.m. They say German tanks are coming this way and that Berg en Dal may have to expect a German bombardment. Called Mr. Fisscher who doesn't think any danger is imminent. I'm going to sing with the girls for awhile; it keeps them together and in a good mood. The children are wonderfully calm.

Wednesday, September 20
The night was reasonably quiet although we kept waking up to the terribly heavy drone of artillery. Since Sunday afternoon there has been heavy fire aimed at Berg en Dal. Unfortunately there are victims, with a shell

fragment hitting the Faasen house right where a woman was trying to shelter a child. The child died instantly, the woman a few hours later. Here, things went well, but we did lose two window panes in the baby house. The glass landed in the bed belonging to Hansje Burger, who had been taken out of it not a minute earlier. Two officers have just come in to advise me to keep the children entirely indoors, as they expect a repeat.

Evening. We did have a small repeat. Mr. Leenders came to discuss our food supply, as he would very much like to see us keep cooking for the thirty-five soldiers in our yard. I told him the stove was too small, and asked if he could get us another one from one of the empty houses left behind by traitors. We're to get one tomorrow morning, along with a few large pans from the hotel.

Thursday, September 21

Spent much of the day bringing in food, as it doesn't look as though regular supplies are forthcoming yet. It was dangerous today, with almost non-stop enemy artillery fire. We're learning to distinguish between the sounds of American weapons and those of the Germans.

Went for milk first thing this morning. Mrs. van Schaik had not been able to milk yet but gave me her last five liters for the children. One of our male refugees will take care of fetching our new stove, and a large suitcase for transporting food.

Saturday, September 23

Thursday we heard the alarming news that German machine guns were at Dr. Roessingh's house, with Americans fighting all around. The same at the van Os place. The Fisscher garage scored a direct hit, and the bad news just kept coming. In the meantime we had to keep things rolling and make sure all 120 people are getting their meals. Terrible news came in from Nijmegen: Anything that wasn't already ruined was set on fire by the Germans. The town of Beek has been cleared again but suffered bad losses. We went to bed Thursday evening but heard deafening sounds of fire through the night.

Friday began well, with Beek and Nijmegen liberated. Flags appeared in town and it was less dangerous to be on the street. The commanding officer in our yard asked me not to send anyone outdoors unnecessarily, as it makes their maneuvers more difficult. I'm permitted through since it's for 'business'. They came to tell us that most of them would be leaving throughout the day. One of our refugee women came up with the generous idea of making pancakes for all the soldiers from her own supply of flour and butter, 130 pancakes in all. Our second stove is working hard. Before three in the afternoon all the boys got a thick pancake as a farewell, but when they were still here at six I made them supper, followed by some soup at eight. After that they did leave. It was not a nice goodbye since we know that these are the shock troops and many of them will die soon. We had become comfortable with them, with their pleasant and polite demeanor. They were grateful for our help and were good with the children.

The commander stayed behind, and today some newcomers have joined him. They fought at Beek and were dead tired. We made an enormous pan of pea soup, and tonight a pan of barley porridge with syrup. They attacked that with gusto. This last group took a large supply of canned food from the Germans, and they brought it here, wheelbarrows full of it. Canned milk, peas, meat, fruit, mackerel, and a crate of sugar cubes. Also raisins, and since I was able to get thirty liters of milk today and got a whole bag of cream of wheat from Mr. Leenders, we will eat cream of wheat porridge with raisins tomorrow.

The Americans don't want much to do with the British. We actually see it too, how the Americans have to bear the brunt of the battle, as they did here with severe losses. Now the British come in calmly to occupy us. The first distressing eye witness accounts are in from Nijmegen.

We're living in total war here. Our thoughts go to our close family members, from whom we are entirely cut off and of whom we know that they are worrying about us. A word of praise for all our workers here. They are doing what they can and staying put. Some of them are moving mountains.

Tuesday, September 26

This past Sunday was fairly quiet, as far as the war goes. We were allocated 25 pounds of meat, so that Leid and I spent the afternoon frying that. The refugees have gone home. Not that they were any bother; on the contrary, they helped as much as possible with food supplies etc. On Sunday, for instance, we received no bread, but Mr. Hamer gave me a big bag of flour.

Monday morning Henny Diks and I ware baking at seven already when the chaplain came to tell us that a group of at least fifty Americans were on the way, and they were ravenous. We gave them what we had, along with a basket of pears and a cup of real tea, which I had received from the commander. Those men were a sight with a seven days' growth of beard, and exhausted. We were happy to be able to refresh them. In the short time they were here they managed to wash, shave and brush their teeth at our rain barrel.

We no longer have a steady group in the yard, just men coming in all day long for food as though we're a cafeteria. I make sure we have a large pan of soup going all day, and a pan of stamppot (potatoes boiled with a vegetable and mashed together) for supper.

Yesterday morning there were two robust young men here that Hélène and Riet brought along from downtown: Dutchmen! One of them had crossed to England in 1939 already, while the other one lived in South Africa for fourteen years and had enlisted from there. They had jumped down here on September 17, and it was their first jump. They had fought in Burma, were back in England for only a few weeks, and had no opportunity to do a practice jump. They were determined to go with the first group to Holland and luckily all went well. They were permitted to do as they pleased for a few days. Of course I invited them for supper. We held a singsong by candlelight that evening in the sun room. Some English boys came too, and the air was thick with Dutch, English, and South African songs. I gave them a comfortable warm bed that night. Although this is not really permitted, the colonel won't make a fuss. In the morning they left well rested and refreshed.

Wednesday, September 27

A phone call yesterday advised me that emergency rations could be picked up here in Berg en Dal, against ration cards. Right now we only get half our bread ration, which is twelve loaves daily for all of us. Since Saturday we get milk again. Yesterday I received fourteen pounds of horse meat, due to all the extra cooking we're doing here. It's all working out and I must say that I'm getting excellent cooperation from all those dealing with the food supply.

We're still fully in the line of fire and no time of day is peaceful. There are many people around here who never get out of their cellars. Yesterday we had a violent aerial battle right above us between the Germans and Americans. The windows flew open from the air pressure and the noise was deafening. Actually we lose windows all the time, but compared to Beek we've been lucky so far.

I was just called into the kitchen, and there was the white-haired commander again. He looked so well rested, and said they had been able to bathe and sleep in real beds for two nights. Although he already thanked us last week with all kinds of foods taken from the Germans, this time he brought a nicely wrapped box of several hundred Chesterfield cigarettes, and a hundred packages of chocolate to distribute among our three houses. The good man must have said a hundred times how much he appreciated the warm food we supplied when they had none.

Thursday, September 28

We have primarily English occupiers now. They're not so bad, and several of them come for a little chat every day. In general they don't seem to have the hate for Germans that we have. I did tell them that they can't imagine what we have had to endure in these years. For their part, they think it's terrible that girls who socialized with Germans are having their hair cut off forcibly, and when possible they prevent it. The Americans also. Other than that, they like Holland and are enjoying the people. They're all very sure of victory and even when things aren't too rosy they remain optimistic.

The situation yesterday wasn't great, and Beek especially suffered badly again. Amidst all the rough acts of war, a baby was born yesterday in Dr. Roessingh's cellar, in the most primitive conditions. The woman and child may be coming here because the cellar there is very small and the whole family is living in it.

Monday, October 2

We're having to be very frugal with candles. Our own supply is exhausted but I'm being supplied by a couple of our English friends. Yesterday we held a church service here for the people of Berg en Dal. There was a good turnout and the minister came to lead the service. The two Dutch paratroopers were present, and this was their last visit as they are going to Germany. Let's hope these brave men will be spared. I was able to treat everyone to a good cup of coffee, which was much appreciated. Saturday night we had a games night for all the soldiers in the area. They like to sing too.

Sunday the news came that the 2nd British Army was entering town. We went to look and sure enough, it was a real invasion. The whole lane here was immediately filled with tanks and other vehicles. Three officers came to see me and requested billeting overnight. We put twenty-eight in the middle house, sixteen in the baby house, and here in the kitchen, another eight. They were all decent guys who caused no trouble and left everything tidy. The main body left at 4.00 a.m. but a few stayed behind to clean up the place. They were picked up by an officer who came to thank us for our hospitality.

This past night was exceptionally dangerous. I don't know whether the Germans knew there was such a strong group here, but from midnight till five we were steadily under German fire. Since I had been warned beforehand, I did not go to sleep, and the big girls were up part of the night too. We survived with numerous broken windows and a grenade strike in the garden, which made an immense bang. We witnessed an aerial battle over Beek and Ubbergen that left several dead and wounded in town.

It's expected that the situation here will be troubled in the next while. We live too near the German border and the Germans keep trying to cross it. Our early expectation of this being a peaceful backwater is proving false. These are nerve-wracking days due to the enormous responsibility we all carry. I'm amazed every day that until now all is going so well with the children. But how much longer will it take?

Monday, October 9

We've been without electricity and water for most of the last week. Since Saturday that has returned, though, and we feel rich. If the gas will come back too we'll be able to take baths, and it will make doing the laundry much easier. However, when we think of the misery suffered by those who are still in the occupied part of our land we just carry on again.

This week was relatively peaceful although the artillery keeps thundering over the town. It seems you get used to anything. We had eight telephone men stay here for three days, then fifteen Scots who had a day of rest. They all stayed in the middle house. They were cheerful boys for whom we organized another evening of song. The next day they left and I thought to finally take a deep breath when a Captain arrived who requisitioned the middle house for office and telephone service. His men immediately went to work to dig an enormous pit in the front yard. The grounds are getting to be a sight, but we'll be able to clean it by spring. They left in the evening for Nijmegen to guard bridges and were to return the next evening. However, on Sunday morning they were back early, took everything down and left in a tremendous rush. Peace has returned.

Had church here again yesterday. The turnout was large, including Englishmen. The coffee afterwards is appreciated and gives the minister a chance to talk with people too. He even provided a brief résumé of his sermon in English. People are relieved to come here. So many are living full-time in their cellars while we live quite normally here. It rescues them briefly from the worries that plague them, and from being enclosed in such claustrophobic quarters with many other nervous people. We consider it a great blessing that we all have our work here, which distract our thoughts from worry.

We held school here for the first time today, with twenty children involved, all different ages. Six of them would normally have begun school in September.

Wednesday, October 11

Went to Nijmegen for the first time yesterday to arrange some financing for this place. The bank manager promised to pay out what is owed me even though there's a moratorium in force. I have to return

Thursday. It was bad weather but that meant the skies were peaceful. The women show more resilience than the men, it seems. The food supplies in the city are not good. We're blessed as far as that goes.

Most of the farmers haven't harvested their potatoes yet, but will have to soon. We've begun with our own garden, and still have more in the field. I was allocated an extra 220 pounds today, a bonus. People do remember us whenever food confiscated from the Germans is available.

Tuesday, October 24

We have water again, electricity, and gas. The artillery keeps thundering over our town and German grenades continue to fall. On Saturday, five people were killed by one grenade, including one man who came to help dig our potatoes.

Our English friends are holding a children's party on Saturday. The major is a competent magician and the children are learning new skits to perform. Next week we'll hold a social evening for the soldiers here in the sun room, with folk dancing and games. That will include all staff, the girls, officers and soldiers. The latter are selected by their officers for good behaviour in polite society.

Monday, November 13

After a fun evening with the soldiers on October 25 we now have a somber report. First of all, Henny Diks was struck by a splinter bomb while in Nijmegen. Her right arm is shattered, a fragment in her lung, and a wound on one leg. The doctors hope to save her arm although it will likely remain stiff. The girl beside her was killed, and there were 150 dead and wounded in all. When I heard of the aerial attack near the Canadian hospital I was worried sick. I asked my English friends to drive me there and after much searching through the hospital's bomb shelters I finally found her. It was a sad tour through the hallways and shelters, overflowing with victims of the war.

The second bad fright came on November 5 when rumours came that we would have to evacuate within three days. I immediately went for official confirmation and alas, it was true. No one knew when or how, at that time. The English were organizing it and they warned us to start preparing. On Monday, November 6, I was told we would be leaving on Wednesday, destination unknown!

We began packing furiously, of course, but that evening our baby house was struck by two grenades. The damage was horrendous, but the important thing is that none of the children or helpers suffered as much as a scratch, which is a miracle considering the destruction of various rooms. We had to move the children by candlelight to our first house. With some English help, the transfer was completed quickly. We had to turn the kitchen and the room next to it into dormitories, and at eight that evening all were asleep. The whole thing went so quickly that the children had no time to realize what had happened.

Of course with all that, our packing was slowed down considerably. It's hard to know what to take along. Every child was assigned a pillow case filled with their own necessities, and I decided the mattresses and bedding should go with us. I told the English office that we would need six big trucks. At 5.00 p.m. Tuesday we had a phone call and the major stood in front of the door with three vehicles: we had to evacuate immediately. That created an upset, as we had not planned for that.

I arranged to have the walking children, school children and the big girls go right then with some of the staff, while I would follow the next day with six of the infants. The whole group would be taken to the monastery at Neerbosch; the next day we would gather them up there and go to the next destination. Tuesday evening and night we worked non-stop, moving all the furniture to a room that would be guarded by the border patrol. I gathered our food supplies into big laundry baskets, which, as it turned out, prevented us from going hungry for the first few days. The major felt bad for us, and it was a terrible situation. We had to leave all our food preserves behind.

Compared to the townspeople we were lucky: they were permitted only a small piece of hand luggage, while we were even permitted to take our clothing. But I'm not exaggerating when I say this was one of the worst moments of my life. Although one house is unusable now, we realized how dear to us were these houses and our simple furnishings. We had to leave our pig behind, and couldn't persuade the cat to come either.

And so we undertook the journey. Our three babies were set into the truck right in their little beds, snug and warm. When we got to Neerbosch all the Gelria inhabitants were waiting for us, and we were happy to be reunited. What a busy place that was, with 2,200 people milling around, and us having to unload our three trucks in the middle of that. All the baggage was taken inside, since we would not continue our trip till evening. They gave us lunch, then were told to take all the baggage outdoors again so that the loading would go quicker when we were leaving again.

It was raining hard, and everything we set outdoors was quickly muddy and wet. We expected the trucks to come then and there, but by six that evening there was still nothing. Then we were told to stay overnight, so we had to lug our mattresses and bedding back indoors, and set them up in enormous halls with many people. The children were great, and amused the crowd with their games before bedtime. They were given three slices of buttered bread and some chocolate milk. Despite all the rushing around we slept fairly well that night. Our English friends from Berg en Dal even dropped by in a jeep to see how we were doing.

Thursday morning after breakfast we were told we'd be leaving in two hours and to get the baggage ready. So we dragged all the mattresses and beds together again but it was several more hours before the trucks appeared. We loaded up again, with the understanding that we were headed for Boxtel to a monastery. We expected to arrive there in half an hour, but no, the trucks headed into the direction of Tilburg. That gave me a really dreary feeling, seventy of us drifting around the roads without knowing where we were headed. At one point we thought to be heading for Belgium, but that turned out to be the wrong road and the trucks went to Brabant instead.

Our final destination turned out to be the hamlet of Lage Mierde, to a labour camp that had been set up during the war for men and boys. The buildings were cold and damp without any heating, and more than primitive. I immediately went to the camp commander and managed to achieve permission to go back to town to the girls' school at the monastery. That was primitive too but at least there is one room with heating, where the seventy of us have to remain all day. We sleep in three classrooms, one for the babies, one for the school children and staff, and one for the big girls, myself and three co-workers. We sleep on straw with our mattresses on top. Good thing I brought all the blankets because it is terribly cold and damp here. Also everyone has caught cold from the trip in an open truck, with much coughing and many sore throats.

The food supply comes from the camp and is very bad. They just can't do it: the town has 88 citizens and then an invasion of more than 1500 people comes in. We get dry bread twice a day with a little milk, and some watery soup or mashed potatoes at noon. Nothing I say is helping, although there are promises of improvement. Nor is there a drop of water to wash with. I went right away to a farmer across from here and arranged to obtain water from there. It's a lot of work but we have no other option. Now our own food supply comes in handy, and we make sandwiches for ourselves. We even cook rye porridge since I had brought our own rye, and I buy ten liters of milk every day from two farmers.

Friday, November 17

It is irresponsible, the way we were evacuated here. Individual civilians from the camp have been billeted with townspeople as much as possible but we have to stay here, devoid of any comfort. I went to Tilburg with Leid yesterday to see if some organization would check up on us, and finally found an inspector of public health who plans to come tomorrow. He is not able to make any promises, however, as the whole refugee situation is bad everywhere.

We have seen a few improvements, though. Although there is no doctor here, there's a clinic on Thursday where we took the little ones. The doctor has decreed that the nuns must cook some vegetables for the little ones every day. We've only had mashed potatoes ourselves, with no vegetables, and have to source any meat, milk, bread and groceries through our ration cards. We now have bread, butter, cooked sausage, and plenty of milk, but no jam, matches, oatmeal, noodles or the like. I'm working on getting a stove here, although placing it will be a challenge. A stove would solve a good many problems. Right now Corry spends all day at the farmer's house to cook our food and heat our water.

It's difficult to get around outside after dark, and we sink ankle-deep into the mud. Two of our staff are sick and the doctor would not permit them to stay here amidst the children. I've been able to arrange for them to be transported to a clinic run by monks. They will be comfortably looked after there by the nurses. Here, it's impossibly noisy and busy with all the children in one room. How long can we keep this up here? It's hard for most of us to stay mentally on top, not surprisingly since I've seldom experienced something this depressing, with endless days.

We did get a bit of a break, with our English friends visiting us. When they heard about the bad food here they managed to return with dozens of tins of meat, soup, fish, and coffee etc. Leid and I went with them to Tilburg, but that's the last we saw of them as they had to go to Germany next. We owe them much for our improved food supply. My family from Eindhoven were also able to visit. They managed to get the use of a car, and when they saw our situation they were unwilling to let Riet and Hélène remain here. I was reluctant to let them go, but it's the best solution for them even though the food supply in Eindhoven is not good either. I did send some along with them, and accompanied them to Eindhoven where I was able to sleep in a good bed for one night. It was only overnight but made a good break for me.

I hate to think we might have to spend the winter months here, with ice and snow and bitter cold. We will have to live by the day and make the best of it. I now realize that Gelria has always been a home for the homeless.

After successful Christmas celebrations for which Clasina Wisman undertook enormous efforts, the order came from the English to evacuate the whole group again, this time to Oudenbosch (Noord Brabant), the next morning. They ended up in two dormitory halls of the St. Anna Pensionaat, a huge, four-storey brick boarding school for girls run by the Sisters of St. Anna. Within four days they were all moved again, to a church hall in Dongen where at least there was running water and some central heating. The food was supplied by a central kitchen run by the nuns; supplemented by their own food supply, Clasina and her brood managed.

Much of Clasina's diary relates her efforts to supply her brood with not only food, clothing, and shelter, but some sense of normalcy. Although Noord Brabant had been liberated, the children's home still lived very much under war conditions. A permit was needed for all travel, while food, fuel, and clothing remained rationed and in short supply.

It is clear that Clasina Wisman was highly respected among representatives of the area's children services. For instance, she was asked to provide advice on how to care for the children of collaborators. The extent to which the Allied occupiers and government agencies cooperated with her requests for supplies also demonstrated her considerable clout. In the meantime she walked thousands of miles in order to obtain what her charges needed. She hitchhiked when possible with military transports, government vehicles, or the rare private cars still able to procure gasoline.

When Clasina visited another children's home temporarily housed in Tilburg, with thirty children sleeping two to a single cot, and even staff members sharing their bed with a child, she noted that her own situation was far more tolerable.

The 'friends' to whom she refers included Civil Affairs, the R.A.F., and the V.H.K. (Women's Help Corps, associated with the Dutch army). These were able to help with supplies and transportation. The British Red Cross even had two mobile laundry units, with another vehicle modified to hold six shower stalls that could be set outdoors but were controlled from within the vehicle.

Clasina and her charges were not able to return to their Berg en Dal home until well after the liberation of Holland. She learned that the two Dutch paratroopers welcomed earlier at Gelria had both survived the war.

Contributors

André Schabracq made it to Paris during the war, and by 1944 worked with the American army to help liberate the rest of western Europe. In 1953 he moved to Canada, where he helped found the Dutch-Canadian DUCA credit union, now the largest ethnic credit union in Canada.

Charles de Greef was born and grew up in Arnhem, where Operation Market Garden took place when he was 17 years old. He moved to the USA in 1953. He worked in liability insurance for 49 years. As a sideline he hosted radio shows in Dutch, on FM, for the Portland region. He lives in Beaverton (near Portland), Oregon.

Anthony van Kempen was born in 1934 in Sint Anthonis, Noord Brabant. He came to Canada in 1948 with his family and has lived in Toronto since 1950. Tony got into the printing business as a messenger boy, and worked his way up to eventually owning a printing business. He and his wife, Annette, have three daughters and five grandchildren.

Liesbeth Boysen-van den Blink was ten years old and living in Eindhoven at the start of the war. After a marriage of 58 years to her husband, Mike, she passed away in April, 2011. She had been living in Bobcaygeon, Ontario, at that time. It was Mike who made her wartime diary available.

Greta Stephany lived in Wolfheze, a small town

near Arnhem, and was eleven years old at the time of Operation Market Garden. She came to the USA in 1956. She is a sister to Pieter Aarsen, also a contributor to this volume.

Pieter Aarsen was born in Arnhem in 1939 and grew up in the nearby village of Wolfheze. He worked for the Dutch railways, served in the Dutch navy, and became a police officer in Rotterdam. In 1966 he married Ellen Ricketts, an American girl visiting Holland. He immigrated to Michigan with her in 1967. They now live in Spencerport, New York. Pieter and Ellen have two daughters and two grandsons. He is a brother to Greta Stephany.

Henk Bosveld was born on a farm near Westervoort, a village near Arnhem, and was fourteen years old when Market Garden began. He came to Canada in 1953 at twenty, and married Hetty van der Stouwe in 1956. He started working in henhouses, spent time as a Fuller Brush man, operated a hardware store, and finally bought a farm. He and Hetty are now retired while still living on the farm.

J. H. (Harry) Caubo grew up near Heerlen in the province of Limburg. In 1958 he followed his Dutch fiancée, Josie, to Miami, Florida, where they were married, with a honeymoon to Cuba. Harry worked with Delta Air Lines and Josie became a registered nurse. They now live in southern Utah in the town of Ivins.

Joseph (Joe) Verstappen was born in Sint Oedenrode,

Noord Brabant. His father worked as a landscaper and grew vegetables for the family's use. Joe was 14 when the fighting at Arnhem began. He and his wife left Holland in 1952, settling in Ontario, Canada. After time in northern Ontario ('too cold!'), they moved to California in 1960. Ten years later they came to Grants pass, Oregon, where they still live. Joe is a tailor and still has customers at the age of 82. He and his wife have two daughters, three grandchildren, and three great-grandchildren.

Josine Eikelenboom was born in Rotterdam and was four years old when the war began. After the Rotterdam bombing, her family moved to Arnhem. There they lived through Operation Market Garden four years later. In 1979 she came to Canada with her husband and children. She lives in Maple Ridge, British Columbia.

John Holthuis's diary was sent in by his wife, Catherina, who lives in Walnut Creek, California.

Henry Niezen grew up in Zwolle, in the eastern province of Overijssel. The war started when he was sixteen. He came to Canada in 1951 with his wife, two days after their wedding. They had four children in different towns, since Henry worked in construction and the family moved all around British Columbia. His four children all received good educations and have worked as an orchestra conductor, a nurse, a professor and a forester. Henry now lives in Victoria, BC.

Jan van Hensbergen was an accountant in Velp, a suburb of Arnhem, when Operation Market Garden took place. His diary was translated and made available by Wilfred Stroeve.

Martha Gubbels-van de Ven lived in Noord Brabant and was eight when the war began. In 1955 her family immigrated to Canada. She and her first husband, Jan van de Ven, had six children before he died. She remarried but was widowed again. The Catholic church in Strathroy, Ontario, where Martha lives, at one time had 40% Dutch members and 40% Portuguese, she says, which means there are lots of Dutch immigrants to socialize with.

Clasina Wisman (1913-1971) was the director of a children's home at the time of World War ll. She had a sister Tiny and a brother, Henk. She had been married and divorced before the war, and had two children of her own, Riet and Hélène, who also lived in the children's home. Sometime after the war she headed the Hervormde Kinderzorgbond, the children's care organization of the church denomination to which she belonged. At that time she was made a Ridder van Oranje-Nassau, a national award that is comparable to a knighthood in England. Clasina Wisman contracted multiple sclerosis at a relatively young age and spent years in a wheelchair before dying in her early sixties.

The Dutch in Wartime series

Book 1
Invasion

Edited by:
Tom Bijvoet

90 pages paperback
ISBN: 978-0-9868308-0-8

Book 2
Under Nazi Rule

Edited by:
Tom Bijvoet

88 pages paperback
ISBN: 978-0-9868308-3-9

Book 3
Witnessing the Holocaust

Edited by:
Tom Bijvoet

96 pages paperback
ISBN: 978-0-9868308-5-3

Book 4
Resisting Nazi Occupation

Edited by:
Anne van Arragon Hutten

108 pages paperback
ISBN: 978-0-9868308-4-6

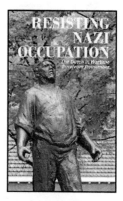

Book 5
Tell your children about us

Edited by:
Anne van Arragon Hutten

104 pages paperback
ISBN: 978-0-9868308-6-0

Book 6
War in the Indies

Edited by:
Anne van Arragon Hutten

96 pages paperback
ISBN: 978-0-9868308-7-7

Book 7
Caught in the crossfire

Edited by:
Anne van Arragon Hutten

104 pages paperback
ISBN: 978-0-9868308-8-4

Book 8
The Hunger Winter

Edited by:
Tom Bijvoet &
Anne van Arragon Hutten

110 pages paperback
ISBN: 978-0-9868308-9-1

Book 9
Liberation

Edited by:
Anne van Arragon Hutten

114 pages paperback
ISBN: 978-0-9919981-0-4

Keep your series complete: order on-line
or contact Mokeham Publishing.

CPSIA information can be obtained at www.ICGtesting.com
Printed in the USA
BVOW08s1006231113

337045BV00002B/3/P

9 780986 830884